LIFT STRATEGIES

Quick Tips to
Engage Customers
and Elevate Profits

JEN DeTRACEY

ISBN: 978-0-9879613-0-3

Library and Archives Canada Cataloguing in Publication

DeTracey, Jen

    Lift strategies : quick tips to engage customers and elevate profits /
    Jen DeTracey.

ISBN 978-0-9879613-0-3

1. Small business—Management. 2. Success in business.
I. Title.

HD62.7.D485 2012   658.02'2   C2012-901350-1

Editorial Services: Catherine Leek of Green Onion Publishing
Design and Composition: Kim Monteforte of WeMakeBooks.ca
Cover Design: Kim Monteforte of WeMakeBooks.ca
Print Production: Beth Crane of WeMakeBooks.ca
Photography: S. Reinier deSmit

Printed in Canada

THIS BOOK IS DEDICATED TO ALL small business owners.

Those who I have never met and those who have worked with me for years. Those who have attended one of my keynotes or training programs.

May all of you make a meaningful difference in the lives of your customers, your staff and anyone else you have the privilege of impacting during your life. You are the leaders of today and the visionaries of tomorrow. I thank you for your contribution to making this world a better place.

FOREWORD

THIS BOOK IS FULL OF VALUABLE, inexpensive, simple and easily implementable ideas and strategies that come directly from Jen DeTracey's real world business experience. They are not hypothetical, complicated or require large investments of capital. Jen understands the culture of small and medium businesses as she lives it almost every day of her life. She sees firsthand what works and what doesn't and thankfully shares it through her client work, keynotes, training programs, and in this wonderful book.

In reading this book, I was reminded of a baseball analogy. Several years ago a study was carried out on the relative levels of compensation paid to professional baseball players. It was determined that a player with a batting average of .333 earned 10 times more than a player with a .250 batting average. That's the equivalent of $5 million to $50 million a year! Yet, the difference in performance is only one base hit in every three games. In other words, a minor improvement but a major gain. That is the message that prevails throughout this book. You don't need to radically change the way you do business. You just need to make minor adjustments in the critical performance areas.

Lift Strategies should be mandatory reading for every owner of a small- or medium-sized business. The format of presenting the information in easily digestible bite-size chunks of information has the added value of making it easy to read and digest. However, the value of the information lies in the using of it. Without implementation, there is no value. I strongly encourage you to take a few of Jen's strategies and implement them immediately. I guarantee that small improvements to your business will result in significant gains.

Norm Friend
Canada's Leading Franchise Expert
Author of *The Complete Canadian Franchise Guide*,
So You Want to Buy a Franchise and *Be Your Own Boss – The Ultimate Guide to Buying a Business or Franchise in Canada*

ACKNOWLEDGMENTS

I WOULD LIKE TO THANK MY fabulous editor/project manager Catherine Leek for her guidance, support and expertise in making this book come to life. Robert Mackwood, my book consultant for providing direction, framework and insights. Kim Monteforte for her creative endeavors as well all others who provided their creative input and contributions, including S. Reinier deSmit for my mug shots, Leith DeTracey (my mom) and Vera Crabbe for their keen eye for proofing.

I would like to thank my good friends, family and colleagues for their feedback, openness to me sharing my process and receiving their support. You have been vital to the life of this book, my state of being – and are too many to name.

To my daughter Nira who I love dearly.

CONTENTS

Part Two

GETTING AND KEEPING CUSTOMERS

Part Three

ADDITIONAL INSIGHTS

THE JOURNEY BEGINS

WHEN MY DAUGHTER CAME home from living abroad in the fall of 2011, it was a short visit – only about five weeks. She was applying for a work visa so she could return to Ireland and work legally in the country she had fallen in love with. In one of our many amazing discussions while we drank tea at the kitchen table, our most relevant and insightful conversation was about how life naturally unfolds.

I shared my career journey with Nira to help her come to terms with her concern of not knowing exactly what she wanted to do with her life and being okay with it. I explained that this discomfort happens and it often occurs more than once in our lives. I took a large post-it note and started tracing out my career path to illustrate where I started and how things had organically unfolded to where I am today. Much of the journey, especially in the early days, was incredibly humbling.

I then mapped out her path so far on another post-it to show where she had started out. The same applied for Nira. She didn't know where she was going or how she'd figure it out when she first left Canada. I posted both journeys on the kitchen wall as a reminder – we don't always know what will happen next but we need to have faith and trust in the process.

At the age of eleven, I fell in love with business and marketing without any conscious awareness. I was working for a company delivering promotional flyers for our local department store, Towers. One day I had the opportunity to triple my income by delivering samples of Aquafresh Toothpaste. This was a new product from Procter & Gamble. No one had ever heard of it before, so I was getting it to "the people" first. There was something very exciting about being at the edge of something new. Luckily for Procter & Gamble, Aquafresh survived and thrived. This was not the case for some of the other products I helped them test in the marketplace.

When I look back at my career history, I can see a common thread. I chose to work for businesses that were in their infancy or toddler years. I was driven to be a part of a team and lead teams of people who where passionate, hungry and motivated to make these businesses successful. I enjoyed the struggle as much as the wins. Working with extremely tight marketing budgets and figuring out how to make things happen became one of my specialties. It meant bringing others onboard to follow a similar vision. It also required a solid plan of action with wiggle room to make changes if things were not turning out as expected.

When I started my first business in 2001, I wanted to focus my attention to help small business owners accelerate their businesses' growth and manage that growth without exhausting people or the resources. I used a tripod approach: working with individual business owners, facilitating training programs and delivering keynotes at conferences and conventions.

The more I presented keynote speeches and training programs to small business and franchise owners, the more I wanted to figure out a way to stay connected with as many of these amazing people as possible. This is when I started to write short, high-impact tips for busy entrepreneurs. These tips took about a minute to read and were free to subscribers twice a month.

As the tips accumulated, I felt it was time to select the best ones, update them and compile them into a book. The purpose of this book is to provide the reader with an opportunity to explore, focus and proactively engage customers and elevate profits.

The book has three sections of quick tips: marketing and systems, getting and keeping customers and additional insights. These tips are based on my personal experiences of working with clients and observing what is happening around me. Although marketing is my leading area of expertise, it is very much entwined with customer service, communication, systems and good business practices. Great ideas only work when implemented properly. Part of the implementation process is getting all the necessary parties to buy into the concept and do what needs to be done to make it happen.

My recommendation for you is to pick a section in this book that interests you or randomly read a number of tips until one hits home. Then come up with a plan to successfully roll it out in a way that fits best with your business model. Allow yourself and/or team to make mistakes and modify as you go. Not everything you try will work. This is where using a combination of patience and gut instinct is important.

Lift Strategies – Quick Tips to Engage Customers and Elevate Profits is geared towards small business owners. Most small business owners, even if they have multiple locations, tend to feel the day-to-day crunch of time to do all that they want and need to get done. This book is a tool that provides ideas and insights, highlighting both costly mistakes businesses have made and shedding light on how they have elevated profits.

After reading this book and by directly applying a number of these proven concepts to your company you will save time and money. Enjoy the journey and remember that no matter how much planning you do, there will always be an element of mystery as to how things in your life and your business will unfold.

Part One

MARKETING AND SYSTEMS

Tip 1

STOP MARKETING

HAVE YOU WORKED WITH customers who actually cost your business money rather than generated a profit?

It does happen. If it hasn't happened to your business yet, then you are an anomaly. The first question we need to ask ourselves when it does happens is, "What am I (and my staff, if you have employees) and the business doing to attract the type of buyers I don't want?"

It starts by understanding who your ideal customers are. From there, pinpoint the characteristics of those clients you don't want to attract. Once you do this, you need to stop marketing to those customers you have no interest in doing business with. This may mean changing the messaging on your website to really hone in on the emotional needs of the customers you love as opposed to a generic message that includes "everyone."

A client of Lift Strategies runs a four-star hotel. One of the challenges they face is not wanting to attract sports teams with lots of young people. While the young people's parents are enjoying the finer things in life at the hotel, such as a nice dinner and drinks in the lounge, their kids are running around in packs having a good time and enjoying their freedom. This scenario presents several challenges. One is the consideration of other hotel guests with regard to noise levels, and another challenge is keeping the young people happy, active and contained to specific areas of the hotel.

Although management has chosen not to turn away young sports teams, it avoids actively marketing to them or putting information on its website to promote or encourage this type of business. In fact, its rates have been adjusted to deter business from sports teams.

What is your company doing to stop marketing to the customers that potentially cost your business money now and in the long run?

Tip 2

IS YOUR MESSAGE MEANINGFUL?

EVER READ AN ARTICLE OR HEAR a speaker who is an expert but they're not willing to share their expertise with you? There is always a string attached. The string is you must sign up for their course, buy their book or tell five friends before you get the golden nugget.

If you want to offer value to your fan club, give them the straight goods. Tell them something useful they can apply right away. Make it meaningful. When you share your expertise, people are more likely to lean in and ask for more.

Take, for example, the insurance business. There is so much information and so many products. It can be quite confusing for the buyer to know what is the right product or service for them. If you offer a regular e-newsletter, blog or website that has success stories of other clients and their situations, then others can wrap their minds around these concepts.

One client I worked with in the hearth industry had subscribers request information on product trends. We built a section into the e-newsletter featuring the most up-to-date product trend information.

When information is relevant to those you are sending it to, the readership and engagement will be higher. Make your messages meaningful and notice the return on your investment increase.

―――――――――――――――――――――――――――――――――――――――(ꞏ)

What type of information would be meaningful to your fans and ideal prospects?

Tip 3

USE LAYERING TO SURPASS SALES TARGETS

WHAT IS MORE DESIRABLE? One pancake or a stack of pancakes with fruit on top? What about a four-layer cake with a light creamy filling versus a cupcake?

Although the stand-alone pancake or cupcake may taste great, the stack of pancakes and the layer cake are certainly more impressive and enticing. Stacking, or "Layering" as I call it, is an important principle when applied to marketing your business. The concept of Layering is the "L" in the LIFFT® Process. I developed this process to help business owners learn to apply effective marketing methods while taking their resources into consideration.

Layering occurs when an organization starts with one method of promotion and then builds on it throughout a 12-month period to create a stronger presence and a greater impact among its ideal prospects and customers. You may begin by sending an e-newsletter to your clients and prospects every month. This would be the first layer. Once this is set up, add another promotional activity to the mix.

The trick to layering is to create a minimum of four to five initiatives (layers) that occur regularly at different intervals. Start with one and then start stacking them as you put each in place.

What layer are you going to start with?

Tip 4

PUT ORGANIZATION ONLINE FIRST

TIME AND TIME AGAIN I HEAR stories about how business owners are too busy to bother with updating or revamping their websites. Sadly enough, it is one of the last marketing priorities for many, yet it is one of the most critical.

As companies evolve, so must their websites. A strong brand presence can no longer be represented by a great-looking business card. With today's demand for information via the Internet, it is time to make sure your organization's website is consistently up to date and effectively speaks to your ideal customers.

I hear stories all the time from graphic design and web development firms that they are too busy servicing customers to showcase the latest projects they have completed on their websites. Wow, this is an oxymoron.

As your small business or franchise evolves, so must your website. It is one of the first points of contact people may have with your business. If this is the case, you want this impression to be current and truly speak to your existing fans and the fans you want to attract.

These days a website is beyond a doubt the starting point to getting exposure on the web. There is so much more to your business, yet your website is your business's foundational starting place. Whether you have one location or many, more and more prospective customers are using their mobile devices right now, this very second, to find out how to get what they want.

Your website needs to be accessible and readable from their devices. Ask your web developer or designer to make sure your business's website keeps up with how users view your information online.

When is the last time you updated your website messaging and visuals to the current standards?

Tip 5
IS YOUR WEBSITE AN ISLAND?

IF YOU ARE USING YOUR WEBSITE as the primary tool for marketing your business, then its core message and the strength of the brand better radiate brilliance.

There was a period of time when I spoke to many business owners and CEOs who invested a good chunk of change and time into their organizations' websites. Despite large investments of effort, time and money, there was a big problem with their approaches. They were missing a step.

This one step prior to modifying or redesigning a website is essential. The first step is to ask the fans what they want.

As a result of not following this first and essential step, these sites ended up lacking a powerful message that spoke from the customer's perspective and in their lingo. Worse yet, there was a brand disconnect between the continuity of the website and all other internal and external communication tools. For some, their brand was either diluted or not integrated wholistically across all aspects of the business. When this happens, it is a costly error.

If you are thinking about changing your website, now is the time to find out what your customers would like to see when they come to your site. Find out what they would like to hear, and what they would like you to offer.

Now is the time to find out why they buy from you and continue to do so time and time again. Those clients who have worked with me to accomplish this goal have built a strong brand presence, have converted more "ideal prospects" to customers and have developed stronger relationships with their existing fans.

Are you taking an all-exclusive approach to developing or redeveloping your website?

Tip 6
WEB DEVELOPER BLUES

OVER THE PAST 12 YEARS I HAVE heard more than a handful of business owners complain about issues they are having with their web designer or the web development company they work with.

The biggest issue is unmet deadlines. Secondary issues are updates to the website and technical challenges that impact the user's ability to use the website as originally intended. If you are like most of Lift Strategies' clients, they depend on their website to be completely up to date and functional in order to conduct business.

One of the ways around relying on your web person for updating in a timely fashion is to move to a content management system (CMS). A CMS enables you or a member of your team to update the website with new content whenever and wherever they are, as long as Internet access is available. This puts your organization in the driver's seat most of the time. Most web development companies can provide a CMS solution.

Secondary issues, such as adding supplementary features to the site or making sure that your organization's website works on different browsers and finicky glitches that can come up from time to time, require your web developer's help. If you are not getting the help you need within an appropriate response time then I recommend switching to another company.

Your website can be an extremely cost-effective marketing tool when it works properly and provides value to your customers. Therefore, you need the best web developer you can afford in order to maintain an effective website.

Are you able to respond to website changes and make timely updates with your existing provider?

Tip 7

BE CONSISTENT BECAUSE THE PAYOFF DOESN'T HAPPEN OVERNIGHT

HAVE YOU EVER EXPERIMENTED by sending out an e-newsletter or mail out and then become discouraged because it received no or a low response? I dutifully sent out my One Minute Marketing Tip e-mail twice a month. At the end of each tip I made a brief mention of a government funded program. After five long months I started to peak small business owners' awareness and curiosity.

When it comes to marketing, frequency is important. People need to repeatedly be reminded that you have something important to offer. Until they need what you have, they won't pay full attention. Don't give up until you have sent your information or promotion out for a period of 9-12 months. This sounds like a long time but in reality it is not. Only 25% of your database will actually open each e-newsletter – and that's an excellent open rate.

Of those 25% of your database who open it, many of these people are not the same people each time so the average contact in your database, with the exception of your fan club, may only read your e-newsletter one out of every eight or ten times that you send it out. This holds true for other forms of promotion as well.

This should help to put in perspective how often you may want to send out your information and to whom. It requires a commitment on your part, or someone on your team, to write the content regularly and get it out there.

With e-newsletters, the frequency of a mail out can be as low as once every three months to as high as once a week. The important thing to remember is to keep doing it. Schedule mail outs so they are sent on the same day every time, on either Tuesday, Wednesday or Thursday between noon and 1:30 p.m. According to Internet marketing expert, Susan Sweeney, this is when most people are more relaxed, are enjoying their lunch or have just returned from a break.

What's your game plan for sending out an e-newsletter with regularity?

Tip 8
DOUBLE INCOME STREAMS

WHEN I ORIGINALLY STARTED my first company, Buzz Marketing Consultants, I recognized that having multiple streams of income was a wise idea.

In the past, I provided consulting services to clients of the Business Development Bank of Canada, taught at Langara College and worked directly with my own clients.

When Buzz Marketing closed and the incorporated company Lift Strategies opened, my philosophy remained firm, with multiple streams of income, including consulting, speaking and training.

In the fall of 2009, after a barrage of media hype on the current economic climate, I noticed many businesses were hit hard with a slowdown in consumer and B2B purchases. Retailers in particular appeared to be suffering greatly.

At this time, my clients trimmed back their marketing spending. Yet, despite working with less marketing funds, the level or intensity of promotion didn't change. At this point those business owners who had more than one stream of revenue experienced fewer problems.

What have you done? Have you diversified your product and/or service offerings? Cut back on your marketing budget? Actively promoted your business more than ever?

I believe the greatest benefit from this perceived recession is the reminder it gave us.

1. Have multiple streams of income.
2. Get creative.
3. Improve customer service.
3. Diversify the product and/or service mix.
4. Promote the best business more than ever.

Which of these five points do you want to start focusing on first?

Tip 9

BE IN COMMAND OF YOUR BRANDS

I WAS CONTACTED BY AMY CROLL from Valadares Law Group in Ottawa. Amy has been receiving my marketing tips since I spoke at an event in Ottawa several years ago. Amy pointed out to me that I was not taking command of all my brands because I wasn't leveraging the power of using the trademark (TM) symbol to identify and protect all the services and processes I had developed. I was writing copy for a new marketing service, the Media Sales Accelerator™ Program, and because of Amy's e-mail it occurred to me that I could incorporate the trademark symbol into the name and take full ownership of the Media Sales Accelerator™ Program.

I'm pleased to say that Amy has very kindly offered to share some basic information about this process.

> A trademark does not have to be applied for or registered in order to carry the TM. This symbol simply demonstrates that you are using the word, name or logo as a trademark and are therefore establishing *common law* rights in your brand. To be clear, the TM symbol can be added to your website and other collateral before applying for formal trademark protection. However, it should be noted that common law rights afford restricted protection and formally registering and protecting your marks is always recommended as an offensive and defensive measure. On the other hand, the ® symbol represents *registered* trademark rights and should only be used once a trademark has been registered with the Canadian Intellectual Property Office. Owning a registration clearly shows to the public that your company values its trademark and has taken efforts to secure the exclusive rights across Canada.

Are you in full command of your brands?

Tip 10

BRAND
SPANKING NEW

I PRESENTED MY KEYNOTE speech, "The 5 Marketing Essentials to Getting 50% More LIFFT®," to an audience of 60 and discovered that at least 10% had concerns that were directly relevant to the subject I was discussing.

These organizations were either going through or had just completed the process of rebranding. Some already had a shiny new logo, revamped business cards and marketing materials. Impressive.

Yet, when I asked, "What are your plans to leverage this new brand to get more business?" it proved to be a difficult question to answer.

Having a new brand definitely feels good, yet on the less glamorous side, it can be expensive both in time and resources to develop. I believe rebranding is a wise investment, but with one important caveat. Having a new brand is only effective if you have an action plan in which to launch the brand into the market in order to gain more credibility, a stronger presence and more ideal clients.

It is not wise to refresh your brand just because you are tired or bored with the one you have. Making a significant change of this nature requires a full-on commitment to share this new brand with your existing customers and ideal prospects in an effective manner.

Before you recreate your brand, I suggest you ask yourself this question, "Do we have the time, energy and money to launch our new brand well?" Start with a rough game plan as to what you will do and confirm this plan is manageable. If so, then go ahead and invest in the revamp. Be sure to have a well orchestrated plan prior to launching it.

Do you have the time, energy and money you need to effectively shift your brand?

Tip 11

RECESSION BREEDS REACTIVITY

IN THE FALL OF 2008, MANY business owners, large and small, experienced a shift in their business. That shift was a decline in revenues.

After talking to a large number of business owners, I discovered that although many of them felt concerned about their present financial situation, they didn't initially respond with a proactive strategy at that time. They decided to ride it out. "Things will get back to normal soon enough" seemed to be their thinking.

The problem was that any reserves they had were depleted and this meant worry for some and panic for others. Those who decided earlier, during the slowdown, to get creative about how to generate more revenue experienced an upward curve within three years. Those who did not now had to play catch up.

If you start actively marketing your business even a little while into a recession, it is very possible that you could still push through a financial slump and come out ahead of much of your competition. Take advantage of the fact that many small business and franchise owners take a reactive approach to marketing rather than a proactive approach. Be proactive during great times and ramp it up slightly when the market starts to slump.

Remember, it is better to begin with a few small marketing initiatives and have them up and running successfully rather than to get bogged down with a long list of great ideas that don't completely get off the ground.

From this day forward, what is the first marketing initiative you are going to make a priority?

Tip 12

COLD BUCKET MOMENT

IN THE SUMMER OF 2008 MY financial advisor hosted an afternoon dessert meeting at her husband's restaurant. She spoke about the markets and what was projected to happen. She recommended that some people may want to move their investments back into cash temporarily or consider transferring high-risk investments to low-risk ones.

Although this made sense to me at the time, I wasn't seeing a dip in my investment portfolio yet so I assumed all would be fine. As a newcomer to high-risk investments (three years in and reaping the benefits big time), I didn't realize that when the crash came, it would wipe out at least 50% of my portfolio within a two-month period. Nor was I aware that it would take more than two years to rebuild or even stabilize my portfolio. As a friend of mine used to say, "This is a cold bucket moment."

While speaking and traveling over the past year, I have spent time with many business owners and managers in towns and cities where the dip in their marketplace hit late. In some cases, it actually just started to take effect in the fall of 2009 or even later. Many of these companies were blindsided just as those of us were back in October of 2008. The sad reality is they didn't prepare their parachute even though they witnessed other struggles in other parts of Canada and abroad.

What I find both interesting, but not at all surprising, is how organizations that worked with Lift Strategies prior to October 2008 bounced back. Sales are strong. A number of these companies had record sales for both October and November 2009. In fact, our own company, Lift Strategies, had its best calendar year to date at that time.

The root of these successes comes down to planning, actively marketing during challenging times and being committed to doing whatever it takes to keep the business on task and on track.

How's your marketing action plan looking for your next business year?

Tip 13

SAYING IT
WITH IMPACT

THE SUCCESS OF YOUR MARKETING activities is based on a number of variables beyond frequently getting you message out there. Although frequency is paramount, it is futile unless you have a powerful core message.

Developing a powerful core message begins with clearly understanding who your ideal customers are – your fans – then communicating a meaningful, high-impact message to them – a message that speaks to their problems with a solution that creates a positive result or change.

Understanding your fans means really digging deep into what makes them tick. The second step in the LIFFT® Process, which focuses on identifying your fans and then developing a power core message, is "Inform." This step helps you identify your number one fans. From there, determine what the core commonalities are between each of them.

Once you get a handle on your beloved fans, you can start crafting the message. This takes time because you need to understand what motivates them to buy your product or service on an emotional level because people buy based on emotions. Come up with as many options as possible, at least three to five, and then choose the one you like best. From there it's time to get some expertise.

Unless you are an experienced writer, consider hiring a copy editor to refine your message so it sounds great, achieves the highest level of impact and leaves your prospects wanting to take action. Hiring an expert to give your message more "pop" will increase the response time and response rate if communicated through the proper channels.

Is it time to refine your message to your number one fans? If so, when are you going to get started?

Tip 14

STANDING TALL DURING CHALLENGING TIMES

PUT TWO BUSINESSES IN THE same industry side by side. Now imagine that this industry is suffering. Despite this, one of those businesses is experiencing growth in the market while the other is barely able to pay the lease. How is that possible?

There are two critical elements linked to business success.

1. Positive Mind-set
2. Marketing Action Plan

If you have a plan but don't believe your business will succeed, the plan will fail. If you have a positive attitude, yet no plan, your business may survive but it won't grow to its full potential once the market sees a positive shift.

If a business is well established and the economy strong, it's easy to get lazy and just reap the benefits of your customers. This is what many businesses were doing before the fall of 2008. When things are not going so well, it can be more difficult to stay positive during challenging times because fear and stress arise. During the 2008 recession many businesses used these circumstances as an opportunity to take a different approach in how they serviced their customers and branded their business. They used this time to re-evaluate and take action.

Those businesses that fell victim to bad times and were not willing to change suffered greatly both personally and professionally.

Aim to have a positive attitude even during challenging times, or at least use the energy you have to fuel positive and proactive change to the best of your abilities. Recognize that having a positive attitude and a solid marketing action plan are a winning combination.

How positive is your mind-set?

Tip 15

GET BIGGER WITHOUT
A BIGGER BUDGET

DO YOU HAVE A MILLION-DOLLAR marketing budget? Most small businesses do not. In fact, most small and mirco-businesses don't have a marketing budget.

For this reason, we must concentrate the focus of our marketing efforts towards the top 20% of our customers – our fans. If you sit down and do a little accounting in your business, you'll find that some 80% of your business revenue comes from about 20% of your customers. Therefore, you'll want to invest your dollars in this crucial category. Maintain your focus on this 20% – don't be tempted to spend your hard-earned dollars elsewhere.

So, the key is to build finely-honed marketing strategies that support this principle. The result will be a bigger bang for your marketing buck.

Who are you top 20%?

Tip 16

TARGET YOUR HOME PAGE

IF YOU GO TO A SHOPPING MALL with department stores, more than likely retailers such as The Bay, Holt Renfrew or Sears have escalators set up to actively direct the flow of customer traffic through their stores.

Ever noticed how the down escalator takes you deeper into the men's underwear department as opposed to the entrance to the rest of the mall?

Are you applying this approach to your website's home page? When visitors come to your business's website it's important to be clear about what you want them to see, do and experience. If your goal is to get them to sign up for your e-newsletter, tip or an interesting article, this offer must be compelling and jump off the home page.

If you are having a sale and you want to drive people to your store, it is critical to feature your sale event prominently on your home page. Make sure to keep your message and brand presence consistent throughout each marketing initiative you are using to promote the sale. This includes leveraging exposure on your company's website to create maximum awareness.

You may have noticed small white squares with a black matrix pattern on them in magazine and on bus shelter ads. These are known as QR codes. The Quick Response (QR) code has become the trend of 2011. Although QR codes have been used in Japan since 1994, North America actively embraced this technology in 2010. When a person scans a QR code with their mobile device, it takes them directly to a specific website page. This is a great way to help a prospect get right to the information they need without having to surf your website to find it.

Get the most from your website. Take charge and direct your visitors into a premeditated action.

How can you use QR codes or home page promotions to drive more business?

Tip 17

ARE YOU SURPRISED?

I WAS WORKING WITH A SMALL business in the skin treatment industry. During the course of the day, we walked through the LIFFT® Process together.

There were several discoveries that often materialize during the course of this 5-Step process. When looking at the list of services this small business offered its clients, we learned some of their services were not very profitable. The company decided to drop these services. When they launched their new website, these services were no longer listed.

In order to invest wisely in marketing for your organization, it is important to review your product and/or service mix. You must be willing to consider minimizing or even eliminating products or services that cost your company money or negatively impact your bottom line.

On the up side, you will have more time and energy to focus on the products or services you know will expand your profit margins. Working smarter not harder is the way to go. When you remain clear and stay the course with what is driving your fans to buy, it's a win-win situation for everyone.

What products or services do you need to drop in order to make your business more profitable?

Tip 18

THE PRICE IS RIGHT

THE TV SHOW THE *PRICE IS RIGHT*® is a household name for many of us. I even bought the game many years ago to play with my daughter.

In the "real world" of business, determining the right price for your products or services can be tricky. From my experience, when businesses are in the infant stage, they stumble in determining the right price based on a balance between profitability and what is fair.

In particular, I have discovered that women who offer services in the healing sector, such as massage or hypnotherapy, often under-charge and over-deliver.

The first step is to be aware of what your competition is charging. The second step is to look at what makes your service or product different and, ideally, better than the competition. The third step is to clearly define each product, service or package of services (bundle) in writing. Write it out for yourself first to work out the details of what you are offering. By doing this you are outlining exactly what your clients or customers will be receiving in exchange for their payment.

In your write-up, be sure to include the actual deliverables – such as a 60-minute massage – as well as all the possible benefits they could receive in return (release of muscle tension, reduction of stress, better sleep at night).

Once you complete step three, determine your costs, such as time, receptionist fees, laundry, merchant fees, massage oil and rental or leasing of space.

At this point, you can then rejig your prices to be in line with your costs and the value you bring through the service or product you offer.

Are your products or services set at the right price?

Tip 19

MORE CONTENT
IS MORE

- Do you want more traffic coming to your company's website?
- Do you want that traffic to come from qualified leads?
- Would you like to get more traffic organically so you don't have to pay the big bucks to make it happen?

WANT TO KNOW HOW TO accomplish these three goals?

Add more content to your website. Make it relevant and appealing to your ideal prospects. This may sound easy, however, we all know that when we rely on our web techie to post new content it could take much longer than we expect it to.

Today I was speaking to an administrative executive and she described how it took two weeks to get one sentence changed on her company's website. Wouldn't it have been faster if she had just done it herself?

Recently, I made the decision to have control over the updating of my site by investing in a content management system that is so user friendly, it's like operating Microsoft Word. These days having a Content Management Site (CMS) is common place.

How does a CMS work? Basically, what I do is go to my website and click on an icon that takes me to a password protected area. I log in, select the page to which I want to make changes, make the needed changes and it's done. I can also add new pages within minutes. In the second phase, the articles section of the website was set up. Each article required me to create a new page. I discovered I could do this in the same amount of time it would take me to contact my web person and ask them to handle it. The result – saving plenty of time and money.

Add more content to your site, do it quickly and see an increase in website traffic within four weeks. If you don't have time to write articles, ask others to produce one and credit them at the end of the article.

What date will you commit to for scheduling at least two new pages of content to your existing website?

Tip 20

WHERE IS YOUR URL?

HAVE YOU NOTICED HOW MANY vehicles have vinyl letters on their rear window or bumper? For small businesses, this has been a great way for them to get exposure wherever they go.

For as low as $50, your website address can become a moving billboard. It's funny when you see beat-up vans or trucks with the name of a company and telephone number displayed on the back of their vehicle. I often wonder if people have the confidence to call these service people after seeing how they take care of their automobiles.

What really caught my attention recently was driving behind a police car. On the back windshield was their URL – *www.vpd.ca* – in white vinyl. When the Vancouver Police Department starts promoting its website on patrol cars, you know you've missed the boat if you haven't already done it.

Taking this a step further, the VPD also communicates to the people of Vancouver via Facebook, Twitter, YouTube videos and even a blog. This is becoming the way of the world.

What's your social media game plan?

Tip 21

SURVIVE THE HIGHS
AND LOWS OF BUSINESS

IS YOUR INDUSTRY EXPERIENCING a serious downturn right now? Are you convinced that this is why your business is taking such a bad hit?

Let's take a look at the real estate industry for a moment. When the market gets tough, only the best real estate agents survive. The agents in the top 20% actually flourish during the lean times because all of the agents who were raking it in during the good times have no idea how to get through when things get really tough.

Is it considered a tough time in your industry? If so, then the first question you need to ask yourself is this, "How good was my organization's marketing infrastructure before things started to go sideways?"

Were you actively marketing during good times? Was your action plan focused on attracting more of the customers you love, your fan club?

If your answer is "no," then do not panic. It may take time for your small business or franchise to redeem itself, but it is possible to shift gears and flourish. The sooner you start the better, because there is no magical marketing pill – too bad, but true.

What's the first step you can take right now towards actively marketing to your fans?

Tip 22

EVERYONE IS A MARKETING GENIUS

IT'S TRUE. PEOPLE LOVE TO come up with great marketing concepts. It's fun.

If you were to take every idea you came up with and write it down in a spiral notebook or record it on your smart phone or digital device, you'd have more than a full night of bedside reading ahead. The challenge is how to best put those ideas into action.

Over the years, particularly during my time as the VP of Marketing for Sarah McLachlan at Nettwerk Records, I discovered that our promotional team had great ideas, many of which were very cost effective. Yet, it was the actual implementation of these concepts that got wobbly. I learned that execution is everything – that and timing.

As business owners, we can't always accomplish this alone. Sometimes it's important to have a business partner, mentor or hire a coach or consultant to be part of the process. Most of the clients I work with, whether they have a business of over $5,000,000 or a sole proprietorship, need help streamlining ideas and developing a game plan. Yet once the game plan is in place, the outcome is best when I walk beside them through the process and help make adjustments along the way. Very few people are able to find the time, energy, focus and motivation when operating solo.

Over the years, I have had mentors, coaching buddies, coaches and worked with consultants to help keep me on track.

Who's helping you stay on track with your marketing strategy and action plan?

Tip 23

WHEN TO HIRE
A PROFESSIONAL

MOST BUSINESS DECISION-MAKERS do not question hiring an accountant or bookkeeper to minimize the amount of taxes owed each year.

The same holds true of legal advice. We don't think twice about hiring a lawyer to handle partnerships, incorporation, trademarks or contracts.

When it comes to designing a new website, we entrust web designers and developers to create and build a high-quality product.

Hiring a small business or strategic marketing consultant is no different. When a business has been running for three years or more, it's often time to focus on accelerating the company's growth. At this point, it's time to hire a professional.

Developing a marketing infrastructure and systems under the guidance of a seasoned expert will save your company both time and money. Through this process the company will be able to respond to new opportunities sooner and secure far more business from its existing customers than was previously thought possible.

In fact, the biggest time-and-money savings come from being coached through a marketing process prior to investing big bucks in a website revamp, new logo or any type of promotional materials or strategies.

Is it time for you to hire an expert to help get your small business or franchise to the next level?

Tip 24

BUILD YOUR FAN CLUB –
ONE FAN AT A TIME

I HAVE BEEN GOING TO THE SAME hair stylist for almost 20 years. He moved to Vancouver around the same time that I did. What's cool about our relationship is that we have seen one another grow in both our businesses and our personal lives. It's a relationship of trust and longevity.

Although I'm not always pleased with every new style he does, I know it will always grow to look great. Mo's clientele has grown so much over the years that I often need to book my appointments three months in advance. For the most part, Mo will not accept new clients unless they are referred to him by the ones he already has because his appointment schedule is so backlogged.

The first time I had my hair cut by Mo was in his kitchen. Then he started working at a well-known hair salon in Vancouver and started to build his client fan base. Over the years he has provided exceptional service and the result has been loyal fans. When Mo changed locations, I followed.

It takes time to build a fan club. It doesn't happen quickly. Overnight success is an illusion that usually comes from many years of building a strong foundation.

When it comes to building your organization's foundation, what are you doing to satisfy your existing customers?

Tip 25

CHANGE IS GOOD

FALL IS A TIME FOR NEW beginnings. Students are back in school, summer holidays are over and many small businesses ramp up into full gear. Fall is also a time of major change. Our company, Buzz Marketing and Consultants, established in 2000, recognized the need to change.

The name Buzz Marketing was conceived in 1998. At that time the term "buzz marketing" was not yet commonly used. Then there was a point where it became over used and now it is simply over. This, married with the changing times, demands for new services and the often perceived dirty words "marketing" and "consultants," brought about a total rebranding process with the help of an amazing design firm called Twin Fish Creative.

As of September 19, 2008, Buzz Marketing and Consultants made the switch to Lift Strategies, Inc.

A great deal of time, work and energy were required to make it happen. Yet, the investment fit with the bigger picture vision I had in mind for the company I was running.

Going through an extensive brand analysis can be helpful in getting clear on what will remain the same with the brand and what will change. I currently know a company that is going through this process and they have decided to keep the same company name and just change the slogan and messaging. Their business has evolved over time and they want to keep up with the times.

In the case of a franchise operation, this is not going to happen, yet you may be actively involved in providing feedback to your franchise corporate office on what is working with the brand and its messaging and what is out of date.

Within your own fan base, you may see ways to switch up your message locally in order to keep up with what your emerging customers want and need. As business owners, once you recognize a need for change you can no longer ignore it.

What part of your brand is falling flat and needs some lift?

Tip 26

NO BUDGET
FOR MARKETING

I WAS CONDUCTING A PRESENTATION on the LIFFT® Process for a local association. During the question and answer period, a successful business owner told me he didn't spend any money on marketing nor did he have a marketing budget. I found this comment very interesting because, over the past 20-plus years as a marketing strategist, I have heard this statement many times.

After asking this business owner several questions, I found out that his company had a website (with professional photography to boot), sent out postcards, and attended networking meetings – all of which cost money, time and energy. All of which are marketing.

What I realized is that often business owners equate the word "marketing" with the word "advertising." Advertising is only one of hundreds of different types of initiatives small businesses and franchises can execute to create awareness. All companies spend money on marketing, even if they get their graphics, photography and printing through barter. If you send out postcards, thank you cards, e-mails or take your clients out for lunch, this is marketing. You have invested in your fans and in your business.

If your company claims to not have a marketing budget, now is a good time to start keeping a record of how much and how often you are investing towards each promotional activity. Include the lunches you or your sales team have with prospects. Until you know how much you are spending and what the return on your investment is, you could be over-investing in things that don't work or under-investing which restricts your company's potential to grow.

How much did you spend on marketing your business over the last 12 months?

Tip 27

PROFESSIONALISM STARTS WITH PROOFING

I AM FACED WITH THE DAY-TO-DAY challenge of dyslexia. Although it may sound like a drag, the truth is that I have learned to be very strategic as a result. Since my early 20s, this has helped me hone my craft as one of Canada's top small business growth experts.

There have been hundreds of speed bumps along the way, and through the lessons I have learned, one of the most beneficial has been to hire others to do what I do poorly. One of the best decisions I have made was to have 90% of my work proofed by a professional proofreader or copy editor.

When it comes to writing sales letters, website copy, promotional copy for postcards or other types of marketing collateral, it more likely than not will benefit from being reviewed by a professional. Unless by chance, you have a person on staff who is an exceptional writer.

There are two areas in which your company can benefit most from hiring a copy editor. The first is with composition.

Have you ever known exactly what you want to say, yet the way you express it on the page is less than perfect? If you can get down the main ideas, even if it's only in bullet form, then this is a good starting place. As long as you have a clear objective for the type of message you want to deliver, a copy editor can assist you with making the message sound great.

The second perk is simply having a professional set of eyes comb through your documents. They can find typos and grammatical errors and polish your document to make it read more fluidly.

When your small business or franchise is able to communicate its message clearly and concisely in a manner that ideal prospects and fans connect with, you will see better results.

Who's helping you craft or fine tune your marketing messages?

Tip 28

MORE FREQUENCY,
MORE AWARENESS,
MORE IMPACT

IN PREVIOUS TIPS, I'VE FOCUSED on identifying your fans, crafting the right message and using the right medium to reach them. The frequency of delivering that message will be addressed in this tip.

Were your marketing strategies over the past year as effective as you had hoped?

If you are going to advertise, you must commit to a regular and consistent strategy for a minimum of 9-12 months. If you advertise for a shorter period, you are wasting your money (unless you are doing an inventory or clearance sale).

This may seem scary to make this type of commitment but here's why it's so important.

Your fans and prospective buyers must be reminded over and over again how you can help them. Until they need what you have they are not thinking about your business, your products or your services. Most people have busy lives and are inundated with marketing messages on a daily basis. The challenge is finding the sweet spot between the time, energy and money you have and the frequency that your fans and prospective buyers can tolerate.

In the case of small businesses and franchises, more often than not, the amount of marketing you do is likely not generating a sizeable demand for your product or service until nearly a year from when you first started.

Frequency applies to all aspects of your marketing action plan not just traditional advertising. It's better to send out a promotional postcard to a small database of fans and/or prospective buyers six times over the course of one year than it is to send out one postcard to a database that is six times the size, only once.

Keep in mind this cardinal rule: More frequency leads to more awareness, resulting in more impact.

What's the best marketing initiative that you can warrant increasing its frequency immediately?

Tip 29

HOW TO SET
ANNUAL GOALS

HERE'S AN EASY PROCESS FOR setting annual goals for your small business or franchise.

The first step is to book time in your schedule to give yourself the opportunity to go into think-tank mode without any interruptions.

The second step is to find a place where you feel most relaxed and focused. Working in this type of environment can be very productive.

The third step in this process is to write down your goals. Without goals, you'll have no idea as to whether your business has come close to meeting, achieving or exceeding your expectations.

The goal-writing process needs to be kept simple. State what you want to achieve as a number or percentage of your sales. Once you have determined this, you can set a date in which each goal will be achieved. Here are a few examples:

- Increase tire sales for XYZ brand by 5% by December 31, 20XX.
- Generate an additional $1,000,000 in sales by June 30, 20XX, compared with the same time last year.
- Grow overall donation revenue by 15% as a result of our legacy campaign by September 30, 20XX.
- Increase Facebook fans by 85% by June 30, 20XX, starting on January 5, 20XX.

Goals that do not have a completion date and a numeric benchmark are not goals. They are most likely strategies. Strategies should not be developed until after your goals are clearly outlined in writing.

What are your top three goals?

Tip 30

THE TRUTH IS IN
THE TRACKING

MANY YEARS AGO, I HAD A CLIENT ask me if it was wise to continue spending $10,000 per year on Internet marketing. I encouraged that client to continue investing this amount and suggested an increase of 25%. My recommendation was based on the results I saw in the client's end-of-year tracking report. The report showed that the client had received the greatest number of inquiries and conversions to sales in the following areas:

- website contact form,
- e-mails to the website's central e-mail address and
- visits to the website prior to any direct contact.

It is essential to track all of your marketing initiatives throughout the entire year. You may be surprised by what's working and what's not. The truth is found in the tracking.

When the clients I work with track the source of their inquiries and sales during a one-year period, it helps both of us to clearly see where to invest future marketing bucks. One of my clients who was quite heavy into print advertising discovered one publication wasn't providing an adequate return on its investment. Although the client was quite attached to this particular weekly paper, it was not getting people into their store.

You and your team work hard for your money, make it work for you. Track your marketing efforts to see what provides the best outcome.

When are you going to start tracking your daily inquiries and sales?

Tip 31

THE 9-MONTH PRINCIPLE

AS ENTREPRENEURS WE ARE often impatient; we want business to fly through the door right now. We think that if we write an article in a local trade publication, attend a few networking meetings and hire a computer geek to boost our website rankings on Google, that will produce instant and fruitful results. This is rarely the case.

I equate the time required before seeing successful results from organic marketing with the time it takes for a baby to come into this world – nine months. A lot happens between conception and birth. This is also true of attracting and retaining customers.

From my experience, it can take up to nine months of attending a networking group before people trust you and give you their business. It can take writing quarterly articles for a trade publication for three issues before the phone starts to ring. It can take sending out nine monthly e-newsletters before you reach your sales targets.

Often, we lose sight of how important frequency is to getting results. We lose perspective because we may have been planning a marketing campaign six months prior to its launch date. In the prospect's mind, however, the promotion appeared for the first time just yesterday.

Commit to regular and consistent promotional activities before you decide whether what you are implementing actually works. Put yourself in the shoes of your potential customer. Realize they are just starting to find out about your business and what you have to offer.

What is the first commitment you will make to the 9-Month Principle?

Tip 32

IF IT AIN'T BROKE, DON'T FIX IT

QUITE SOME TIME AGO, I completed a marketing assessment for a company that had developed a series of low cost ($5.95 – $19.95) products that were selling quite well online. They contacted me because they wanted to dramatically increase their sales, launch a new line of products and explore new markets.

Like many companies in their infancy, this business had invested most of its capital in new product development, manufacturing and packaging. Although the new items looked great and were soon to arrive, the company did not have available funds to invest in marketing these products, nor did it have a marketing action plan.

Through the assessment process, we were able to conclude that deviating from what had made the company successful so far was a costly mistake. Up until that point, this company organically grew its business and needed to continue doing so until it had the funds to step into the mass marketing arena. As a result of our discoveries, we built a set of new marketing strategies to support their existing structure without stepping outside of their financial realm.

If your organization's current marketing and promotions are working, don't stop just because you are bored with your endeavors, or think there is a better way. Take what you are presently doing as far as possible before changing course. I believe many organizations prematurely shift their focus away from existing growth, while money is still on the table waiting to be tapped into.

What marketing initiatives are currently working really well for you?

Tip 33

DOUBLE-DIGIT GROWTH

ON CANADA DAY, I ATTENDED A really great house party. For me, what made the party such fun were the people I met. I didn't know most of the guests, yet I had some wonderful conversations because people were so friendly. In this case, the conversations focused on dating, relationships and business, all topics I enjoy hearing stories about.

One of the conversations was with a dynamic woman who works for Lululemon in a management capacity at their head office. While discussing the economy and how retail was experiencing an overall dip, she said this wasn't the case for Lululemon. In fact, Lululemon had been experiencing double-digit growth. This means instead of achieving 7% annual growth, for example, their stores are achieving 14% or more.

I asked her what the main reasons were for this incredible success story other than obvious factors such as Lululemon's exclusive brand. It seems that women's luxury apparel was doing well, so being in the right industry at the right time had certainly been helpful.

And with that, Lululemon continues to produce high-end products at premium prices. The owner, Chip Wilson, is an outside-of-the-box thinker and an innovation master with a solid team behind him to successfully develop and implement his strategies. Lululemon marches to its own drum and is not swayed by what other businesses are doing. They continue to be a leader in the marketplace by consistently doing things differently than their direct and indirect competition. This keeps their brand fresh, exciting, unique and, most of all, profitable.

What are you doing to keep your brand fresh, exciting, unique and profitable?

Tip 34

MAINTAIN AND GAIN

AS WE MOVE FORWARD WITH OUR businesses, there may be some challenging times ahead. During times of economic instability, it is not uncommon to review present expenses and decide what should remain and what just has to go.

Before you make any big decisions regarding your investment in marketing, I think it is important to share some critical statistics with you.

> McGraw Hill researched 600 companies that either increased, maintained or reduced their marketing expenditures during a previous recession. Those companies that maintained or increased their marketing exposure during the recession averaged a 275% increase in sales during the third year following the recession.
>
> In contrast, those companies that reduced or eliminated their advertising showed only a 19% sales increase during the same period.

During times where you need to become leaner in how you do business, it's important to find ways to continue to reach out to your existing customers and gain awareness with potential prospects. There are many ways to do this without spending heaps of money.

What are three to five low- to no-cost marketing ideas you can implement to maintain awareness for your small business or franchise?

Tip 35

E-MAIL RANT

IT'S NOT VERY OFTEN THAT I RANT about something, so hopefully it won't offend you.

When I do presentations and workshops, I ask the participants if they would like to subscribe to my tips. Most do. Upon receiving all the business cards, I am constantly surprised how many business owners have a website, yet their e-mail address is not an extension of their website address. In fact, there is often very little continuity.

For example, let's say Joan Smith owns a flower shop called Flowers on Demand and her business's website address is *www.flowersondemand.com*. Yet, her e-mail address is *Joan.Smith@yahoo.com* or *Joan.Smith@gmail.com*. This gives me the impression that she doesn't take her business that seriously. Instead, if her e-mail address were *info@flowersondemand.com* or *joan@flowersondemand.com* then I would have a more favorable impression of her business as being professional and credible.

My recommendation is simple. If you have a website address – even if it is not yet active – ask your tech person (if you can't do it yourself) to set up an e-mail address with the same extension as the website address. It makes a more professional, credible, and lasting impression.

What is your e-mail address?

Tip 36

BE SUCCESSFUL IN EXPANDING OR SELLING YOUR BUSINESS

ARE YOU AT THE STAGE IN YOUR business ownership where you would like to sell your company and retire? Or, on the other hand, are you motivated to open up a new location?

Either way, it is important to have your marketing house in order. What does this mean?

From a brand perspective, it is important to have a strong brand and a strong brand message. If you want to sell, your business will be worth more if your brand stands out from your competition and has a perceived high value. If you want to expand from one location to two, or are planning on multiple locations, the brand of your flagship location needs to be solid. If your brand is murky, then it will make adding new locations or selling your business more difficult.

Buyers also want to be confident in knowing you have a solid marketing plan and are successfully implementing this plan with a good return on your investment. It will make their job easier if they can follow your plan with small amendments.

In terms of growth strategies for your business, you will be more successful as you expand if you fine-tune your marketing activities prior to opening new locations. With a strong, tried-and-true marketing strategy, you can reduce the risk of failure in expanding your business and be better prepared for the next phase of your company. Additionally, you can plan for a growing return on your marketing investment.

Are you working a plan that will leverage the value of your business or businesses?

Tip 37

SYSTEMS MAKE OR
BREAK SUCCESS

I SENT OUT ONE OF MY TIPS IN its draft form instead of the final version by mistake. At the time I felt embarrassed because there were several typos in the draft version. And because this tip was sent to a large database of business owners and decision makers, I felt particularly uneasy. My saving grace was that when I realized the error, I recognized the importance of creating a better system that would guarantee this situation not be repeated.

How many times have you sent an important e-mail to someone and then realized after sending it that you had made a mistake?

Or how many times has your company run an ad only to have someone point out a typo once the ad was in print?

Or even worse, how often have you sent an invitation asking clients to a special event but failed to include all the "important" details, like the time or location?

Unfortunately, these things happen and when they do, it's best to get over ourselves as quickly as possible – and then develop a system that will remove the possibility of this happening again.

Although, human error does not make any system perfect, it definitely reduces the probability of error and increases your business's professionalism.

What system will you put in place over the next seven days that will ensure greater accuracy?

Tip 38
WATCH OUT FOR BAD SIGNS

DOES YOUR BUSINESS HAVE ANY bad signs?

In the mornings I walk by a beautiful, green, heritage-style house that has been on the market for about two months. The one thing that grabs my attention every time is the real estate sign on the front lawn.

The sign is attached to an attractive white wooden post, yet what I find to be a real turnoff are several lines of bird droppings covering the sign. Although this may seem like a trivial detail to some, I do question the credibility of the real estate agent who represents this property. Over the past month, the agent has not come around to clean the sign, nor has the home owner.

In my mind it makes the listing look old and reflects poorly on both parties. I experienced a similar situation with a real estate agent who listed my property. He did not trim the tall, wild grass around the sign that directed drivers to the property from the highway. The sign was barely visible until the surrounding grass was trimmed. When this agent's contract came up for renewal I found someone else to represent the property.

Whether your business's first impression to its prospective buyers is a sign, website or the way your team answers the phone, this initial point of contact must be presentable and professional. Recognize your weak spots and improve upon them. Great first impressions count as cash in your bank account.

Do you have any bad signs that need to be fixed?

Tip 39

TUNE IN TO AFFORDABLE MARKETING

THIS YEAR I'VE HAD THE PRIVILEGE of presenting and training in smaller business communities in British Columbia and beyond. What I love most about traveling to the smaller cities and towns are the amazing people I've met and lessons I've learned.

In places like Fort Saint John and Terence, business owners can afford to include radio advertising as part of the marketing mix. What may cost between $13 and $22 per spot in these smaller communities would be $100-$250 per spot in large city centers like Vancouver or Toronto. Although the reach and listenership is substantially less outside of Vancouver, Toronto or Montreal, reaching the audiences in small cities and towns can be very effective.

Radio is a unique medium in which a story can be told. This is different from print, direct mail or Internet marketing. If your local radio station reaches your ideal customers and costs less than $20 per spot, you may want to consider it as one of your marketing layers.

Remember, you first need to know who your ideal customers are and confirm that the radio station you are considering broadcasts to the people you want to reach. Once you are able to confirm this, then talk to the sales rep to determine what type of exposure you can get to build brand over a 9-12-month period. You might be surprised at how many new and repeat customers you get walking through the door without breaking the bank.

Is radio advertising a viable option in your market?

Tip 40
BRAND YOUR RULES

WHILE VISITING MY SISTER ON the Sunshine Coast, I was hanging out in the kitchen making breakfast. Every time I went to the fridge, I would scan it to see what photos caught my attention.

On this particular morning, I noticed a postcard from the Gumboot Cafe that laid out the "Gumboot Rules." After reading them over, I wanted to share them with you:

1. The best things in life aren't things.
2. Never judge a day by the weather.
3. Tell the truth – there's less to remember.
4. Speak softly and wear a loud shirt.
5. Goals are deceptive – the mis-aimed arrows never miss.
6. He who dies with the most toys – still dies.
7. Age is relative – when you're over the hill, you pick up speed.
8. There are two ways to be rich: make more or desire less.
9. Beauty is internal – looks mean nothing.
10. No rain, no rainbows.

The Gumboot is a restaurant and cafe in Roberts Creek on the Sunshine Coast of British Columbia, Canada. It makes most of its meals using vegetables grown from its own garden. It's a funky place with earthy culture and brand. The owners and their staff know who they are, and so do their fans.

Is your business's culture and brand crystal clear to you, your team and your fans?

Tip 41

DO YOU HAVE BUY IN?

EVERYONE WHO OWNS A BUSINESS has good marketing ideas. The implementation can be another matter altogether.

When we sit down with a business owner to discuss or brainstorm a new concept, we take the time necessary to discuss how feasible it is to implement. In our next meeting we revisit the concept. Often, the client's first question is, "Can you tell me why we are doing this?" There are three reasons why this question comes up.

1. Fear of doing something new or fear of failure
2. Not understanding the benefits of moving forward
3. Lack of buy-in

The third reason, lack of buy-in, is the result of the first two reasons. If the business owner has resistance to a new concept and is unable to buy into it, then the idea will most likely fail. This is because it is the owner's responsibility to believe in the concept and be passionate when communicating it to their team. If the team doesn't buy into the concept and the game plan, then it definitely will fail.

Are you committed to energizing your team every time you implement a new marketing initiative?

Tip 42

IS YOUR BUSINESS
IN FULL BLOOM?

I AM BY NO MEANS A GARDENER. In fact, I don't really like to get dirt in my nails. So I guess I turned a new leaf this year when I decided to plant four sunflowers in front of my house.

Although there was a garden area with a big rhododendron bush, the rest of the garden under my front window was merely earth and a large rose bush. I have a friend who is an avid gardener coach me on how to grow and keep these little seedlings alive and healthy.

The three basic essentials were sun, water and support. I couldn't guarantee the sun but I did set up stakes for each flower and water them regularly. As are result, I witnessed these beautiful flowers bloom. Incredibly all four had multiple flowers. Some would die and then others would bloom.

There was one mystery for me. The leaves that hung from each stem where either dead or dying. I didn't understand why until I asked my friend.

The issue appeared to be the soil; the soil in which these beautiful flowers were firmly rooted was terrible. It contained very few nutrients. So even though I was giving good care to each plant, I had not dealt with a very important factor – to properly nurture my sunflowers.

To me this analogy is similar to how we as business owners manage our businesses. If we don't prioritize the foundation of our company or organization, by having a solid marketing action plan in place or making sure our team is behind our promotional efforts, we will not get the best results. There may still be a positive outcome but full potential will not be achieved. In the end, taking a little extra time to put the pieces in place can result in an exponential outcome over time.

Next year if I decide to plant sunflowers again, I will definitely start them off with a new bed of soil so they have the potential to grow and flourish fully.

———————————————————————————————————————(ᴵᴵ)

How solid is your business's foundation?

Part Two

GETTING AND
KEEPING
CUSTOMERS

Tip 43

PICK UP
THE PHONE

ONE FRIDAY AFTERNOON MY Internet connection was down. As you can imagine, this was very frustrating. I had to rethink my entire day once I discovered the problem would not be resolved until Saturday.

I was eventually able to receive incoming e-mail through my webmail, but still unable to send out. In my webmail I found some extremely important personal and business e-mails that needed immediate attention. Of course, I received these at the nth hour, as I was trying to finish up so that I could head to my cabin for the weekend. So what did I do? I picked up the phone.

When I do not hear back from a client or prospect to whom I've sent an important e-mail earlier in the day, I don't hesitate to pick up the phone and call them. I believe as a society we have become too dependent on texting – and e-mail in particular – as our primary form of communication.

Earlier in this particular week, I was speaking to a successful book publishing sales representative. He expressed how it was so much easier to have a quick and effective conversation with a prospect and get all their questions answered during a phone call rather than to go back and forth multiple times by e-mail.

I agree. If you have a business, you are in the relationship business. This means a balance of e-mail, texting, in-person and telephone interactions.

When is the last time you picked up the phone?

Tip 44

BUILD A LOYAL
FAN BASE

BACK IN THE EARLY 1990s I WAS the marketing director for Sarah McLachlan's record label. One thing we focused on was slowly and steadily building up Sarah's fan base through newsletters, mail-order sales and an exclusive fan club.

Building your fan base starts with asking, "What can I do to tell the customers I love how much I appreciate and value their business? And how can I do this in such a way that it gives me an advantage in the market place?" This was my mantra.

Those of you who worked, lived or visited Vancouver between 2007 and 2009 are fully aware of the construction along Cambie Street in order to build a new subway system prior to the 2010 Winter Olympic Games. It greatly impacted businesses in the Cambie area. Not all enterprises were able to weather the storm. Those businesses that were established and had a loyal base of customers – a fan base – were more likely to survive. Their customers came and bought from them despite having to take five detours and drive down a few back alleyways. I did. However, those businesses that did not invest their marketing dollars and time wisely, at least two to three years prior to the construction, struggled and many of them were faced with moving their business, closing it or even bankruptcy.

Be smart now. Build a loyal base of fans while your business is growing and strong. Things can change in an instant. Unexpected events can take place overnight so you need the security of knowing your core customers will stick with you even through difficult times.

What's the first step you are going to take to build your fan club?

Tip 45

HOW DOES YOUR
BUSINESS SMELL?

THIS MAY SOUND LIKE AN ODD question if you are not the owner of a spa, bakery or restaurant, but it does reflect an important question. Since branding is a full-on experience, this may be something you want to consider.

Our company, Lift Strategies Inc., is a sponsor of a franchise event called the Franchise Forum. The Franchise Forum's last guest speaker was Brian Curin, the President of the Flip Flop Shops®. Flip Flop Shops® is the authentic retailer of the hottest brands and latest styles of flip flops and sandals.

Just as you enter Flip Flop Shops® anywhere around the world, you will experience the delicious – and distinctive – scent of coconut. This scent lingers as you go in and then blends into the background as part of the consumer experience. The vibe of the Flip Flop Shops® is to give the consumer a "mini-vacation" experience while in the shop.

According to Brian, research has shown that when people smell a similar scent at a later date, they are likely to equate it with an earlier experience. The scent of coconut may give shoppers a flashback to their visits to the Flip Flop Shops®. Is that cool or what?

As part of a coconut-scented reinforcement, Flip Flop Shops® sells its exclusively branded coconut-scented lip balm for only $3.

What does your brand smell like?

Tip 46

MAINTENANCE MARKETING

WHAT IS IT? MAINTENANCE marketing is when your small business or franchise reaches out to its existing customers on a regular basis beyond sales calls and problem solving.

More often than not, once business owners put their focus on getting new customers, they neglect marketing to the ones they already have. While the customers you have may only buy from you every five years due to the nature of your product or service, they can be an excellent referral source. If they buy from you regularly, not only can they also be a great referral source, they have the potential to buy more and buy more often if you stay connected with them.

It is important to build several maintenance strategies into your weekly and monthly marketing activities to reach your existing customers. Connecting with your fans on a regular basis is like discovering gold. Even if your product or service is one that does not get purchased very often, the people who do purchase it will be keen to share their experiences, good or bad, with others.

Maintaining your connection with these customers is vital, especially in an economy where customer loyalty is more challenging to uphold.

What can you do to stay connected with your #1 fans at least four times a year?

Tip 47

ALLOW YOURSELF TO SAY "NO"

THERE WAS A TIME WHEN I WAS speaking to and corresponding with a prospect that no longer fit my ideal customer profile. I broke my own rule. The result was a great deal of time spent on my part communicating with an individual who was either a procrastinator or did not make the final buying decision, despite indicating that he had license to make these types of decisions.

Yesterday, he asked me if I wanted to go for coffee and I said, "No." I told him that I usually work with companies that are much larger and are ready to take action. I finished by saying, "When you are ready to take action, let me know."

When we look at everyone as a potential customer, we really limit our business success and waste unnecessary energy. Few of you reading this marketing tip are likely to have a million-dollar budget to spend on marketing to "everyone."

Look at your business as it is right now. Who are the customers you love to do business with? Who are the customers who buy your products and/or services over and over again, pay what you want to charge and are mutually respectful?

These are the customers to whom you want to say "Yes." These are the types of customers you want to categorize by industry, personality, revenues, demographics, etc., so you can effectively select the appropriate promotional methods and invest your marketing dollars efficiently in keeping these ideal customers as clients and generating more of the same.

Who are the prospects you need to start saying "no" to?

Tip 48

SIMON SAYS COPY YOUR COMPETITION

WHILE TEACHING MARKETING FOR Managers at Langara College in Vancouver, I remembered showing a video to my students about setting the right price. There were two key points that resonated with me.

The first is to avoid copying your competitor's pricing model for the sake of following the leader. When setting the price, you need to ask yourself, "Do I know if my competition's pricing model is profitable?" Assuming it is could be a costly mistake.

The second point addresses the risk of positioning your company as the "lowest" or "best" price. When your organization goes with the "lowest" price strategy, you make it impossible to develop brand loyalty among your customers. As soon as a competitor enters the market with a lower price for the same product or service, you're hooped.

Going with the lowest price for short-term gain will cause you long-term pain. Your pricing strategy needs to represent the complete experience and benefits that your customers will receive before, during and after they make their purchase.

What is a fair price for your products or services based on how you want to be perceived in the market?

Tip 49

MAXIMIZE YOUR EXISTING CUSTOMER PURCHASES

FOR THE PAST THREE MONTHS, I have been working with The Vancouver International Fringe Festival (*www.vancouverfringe.com*), one of the top festival organizations in Vancouver. The Fringe offers a diverse roster of theater over a ten-day period. Lift Strategies was hired to help management come up with a number of strategies to maximize sales using their ticket sales database.

While working with the executive director, I recommended we launch a 72-hour campaign targeting the "Fringe Addicts," a very specific Fringe audience. A Fringe Addict is a festival-goer who has attended five or more performances during at least one festival over the past three years.

The campaign was also focused on promoting the Vancouver Fringe's biggest kick-off event, the Gala Opening, which took place the day before the festival commenced. What we did was exclusively offer the Fringe Addicts an item that was not for sale: the infamous festival T-shirt, which would be offered as a value-added item if they purchased tickets to the Opening Gala through the online ticket system within a 72-hour period.

Because frequency is what gets results, three e-mails were sent over the course of the 72-hour promotion. The first announced the campaign; the second was a reminder; the third stated the cut-off time for the promotion. It was no surprise that the final e-mail generated the greatest ticket sales.

Tickets sold as a result of this promotion represented 7% of the entire Fringe Addicts database. This percentage for e-mail-driven campaigns was well above the average conversion rate of 0.5-2%.

What exclusive offers or opportunities are you providing to your #1 fans?

Tip 50

EMERGING FANS
ARE THE FUTURE

FROM THE ONSET, WHEN CLIENTS work with me they discover that our initial focus is to dial into identifying their number one fans. Those are the customers who love working with you and, likewise, you love helping them.

Upon digging deeper, clients and participants of my training programs and keynote presentations often discover they have more than one category of number-one fans. Hence, the term "groupies;" having more than one group of number-one fans.

Once all marketing efforts are in place to attract more number-one fans and keep them coming back for more, it's time to focus on the *emerging* fans. An emerging fan is a customer group that has great potential of becoming number-one fans.

Let's say you own a jewelry store. Your number-one fans are baby-boomer couples who live a middle- to upper-class lifestyle and love jewelry as an annual gift from their spouse. An emerging customer may be the couple's adult children who want to get married and need engagement rings. These emerging fans are not regulars to the store, yet they know their parents have been regulars and they, in turn, decide to purchase at the same place. Once they make that initial purchase, they may become loyal fans if you are able to maintain a long-term committed relationship with them over the years as they grow older and celebrate more special occasions.

If you feel you are totally on track marketing to retain your existing number-one fans, then it's time to start exploring who and where your emerging fans may be. After all, your emerging fans are the future of your business.

Do you know who your emerging fans are?

Tip 51

STEP OUTSIDE YOUR INDUSTRY

ONE OF THE BENEFITS OUR CLIENTS get from working with Lift Strategies is that the client work we do spans a broad range of industries. Why is this helpful?

When we meet with a client initially, they will share with us what types of marketing activities they are doing and how it compares with what others are doing in their industry.

I believe one of the best ways to be a leader in your industry is to step outside of the box and take a more varied approach to marketing over your competitors. One reason for this is that the arena your competitors participate in may be overcrowded.

Often, companies keep with the marketing techniques they have been using for years without properly evaluating whether these methods are still effective. One of the best ways to get around this, once you have done diligent assessment of what is presently working for you and what isn't, is to step outside of the your industry's box.

I recommend you take a look at what other industries are doing and see if it makes sense to apply a few of those concepts in marketing your business. You may be surprised at the number of ways you can increase your business's presence in the marketplace without overstretching your resources.

For example, it's not uncommon to see fast-food restaurants hire young adults to dress up in funny costumes and wave signs on a street corner. One of my clients was having a sofa bed sale during the summer months, but their location was tucked away off a busy street. We ran a weekend campaign where they set up an open sofa bed on the corner of the sidewalk and two young adults invited people to join them in bed. When passersby sat or laid down in the bed, they received a card for a free gift at the store – no purchase necessary.

The response to the promotion was very positive and the awareness they created for the sofa bed sale was phenomenal.

What marketing concept can you reference from another industry and put your own spin on it?

Tip 52

ESTABLISHING GREAT
SPONSORSHIP AGREEMENTS

LATELY I HAVE BEEN WORKING with clients on developing sponsorship agreements that rock.

What is a sponsorship agreement? To me, it is an agreement between two organizations in which both gain benefits and meet specific objectives.

Simply put, festivals of all kinds – including music, theater and film – are prime examples of organizations that seek sponsorship. They are often looking for suppliers who can contribute money, sound equipment, printing, catering, beverages, advertising, prizes and media coverage.

I believe sponsorship works best when the audience of a festival gets to truly experience the sponsor's product or service. One way to achieve this objective is through providing product samples to the audience.

Several years ago, we wanted to increase ticket sales for the gala opening of Vancouver's International Fringe Festival. One way in which we achieved this goal was by providing $25 goodie bags filled with cool stuff, including a beer glass, handmade card, chocolate and tea.

If you are considering entering into a sponsorship agreement, ask yourself, "What is the best way to create an experience for the customers, patrons or audience that will provide a lasting impression?"

Partnerships with other businesses or organizations can work similarly. Look to industries you want to be connected with and find out how you can each gain exposure and experiences with each other's customers.

What type of partnership or sponsorship would give your business great exposure?

Tip 53

GIVE YOUR PROSPECTS MORE THAN THEY ASK FOR

DOES YOUR BUSINESS FOLLOW A model in which you provide a quote, estimate or proposal to your prospective clients?

When you (or someone within your organization) write up this information, do you give the prospect exactly what they asked for or do you offer them more?

I learned the following strategy from Alan Weiss and would like to share it with you. Based on my personal experience, it works.

After meeting with a client, draw up a proposal based on your communication with them. Then ask yourself, "What else can I offer that would greatly benefit this prospect?" Keep asking yourself this question until you come up with at least three proposal options:

- Option One – what they asked for
- Option Two – what they asked for plus more value
- Option Three – what they asked for plus more value beyond Option Two

You may be uncomfortable when you read this and feel it is wrong to take this approach. You need to understand that prospects are talking to you because you are the expert at what you do. You likely have more insight into how you can help them than they do. It is your responsibility to provide them with all the options and then leave it to them to choose which option would benefit them the most.

Invariably they may surprise you by selecting option two or option three. Try applying this concept both to your ideal prospects and your existing customers.

Are you educating your customers about the depth of products and/or services you can offer them?

Tip 54

PREMIUM PRODUCT, PREMIUM PRICE

WHO ARE YOUR NUMBER ONE customers? I'm talking about your fans, those customers whom you love and those who love you. These are the customers you want to clone and, if you could, you'd have your cloning laboratory up and running in a nano-second.

When you take a really hard look at these fans, are they just like you? They may be, but it's possible they are not. What about your front-line staff who connect with these fans daily? Are they generating a similar income as your fans? Are they driving the same type of vehicle or living a similar lifestyle? Often this is not the case. For example, employees who work in jobs at high-end restaurants, spas or house cleaning services are not likely to be in the same financial position as those who are paying for these services. I know there are exceptions to this rule.

If there is a moderate to big gap in the lifestyles of your front-line staff and your customers, how do you and/or your team develop a true understanding as to what is important to your number one fans? Getting a great bargain is rarely the customers' number one concern. Getting around this thinking requires you to put yourself in their shoes.

If you offer a premium product or service, then your pricing needs to be premium. As soon as there is a disconnect between the caliber of the product compared to the price, there is customer confusion. Take the time to fully discover the values, beliefs and lifestyles of your fans. Once you do this, be sure to communicate this information, educate your team and, even better, make them a part of that discovery process.

The outcome is better customer service, higher profits and happier customers.

Does your team understand who your #1 fans really are?

DOWNSIZE YOUR MESSAGE

HAS YOUR BUSINESS BEEN negatively affected by what is happening with our economy?

Whether your answer is yes or no, now is the time to downsize your message. One of the greatest mistakes made by businesses and organizations is to scramble for more business without zeroing in on a specific area of opportunity.

At this point, the money you invest into your marketing initiatives needs to generate positive results. The first step before conceptualizing great marketing ideas is to ask yourself this question, "Which is the best group of customers or clients to target right now?"

When we jump right in without clarifying to whom we want to sell, we are wasting valuable time and money. Start by looking at who your best customers are right now. Ask yourself or your team, what they have in common and what motivates them to buy your product or service. Once you nail this down, then you can draft a compelling core message that speaks directly to these prospective buyers.

The more you clarify who this group of ideal customers is – your fans – the more likely the message you create and action plan you develop will be successful.

By downsizing your message, you end up speaking to a select group of individuals who quickly become aware of what your small business or franchise has to offer and how it will benefit them.

Which group of customers will you focus on right now?

Tip 56

ATTRACT MORE CUSTOMERS

HERE ARE THREE REASONS WHY advertising doesn't work.

1. Wrong or irrelevant medium
2. Wrong message
3. Lack of frequency

How do you know which newspaper, magazine, radio station, online directory or association to advertise with?

The first and most fundamental consideration in selecting the right type and form of advertising is to understand who your ideal customers are. Not everyone will be interested in purchasing your product or service. The 20% who do, and consequently are the ones that generate 70-80% of your total annual revenue, are your fan club. They are the ones from whom you want to generate more business.

Identifying your fan club helps to determine the demographics (i.e., age, gender, single, married, income, etc.) and buying behaviors they have in common. Once the fundamental demographics of your fan club are clear, your marketing and advertising efforts can be honed to become 100 times more effective.

If you can afford to carve out a marketing budget and are able to commit to investing in a medium that speaks to your fans and potential fans for at least a 9-12-month period, then you can move to the next step. Develop a powerful headline or message that directly engages your fan club prior to committing to buying an ad.

When you successfully combine the right advertising medium, the right message and the right frequency, you will get the biggest bang for your marketing buck.

Are you reaching your #1 fans with the right message, with the right medium?

Tip 57

ANYONE AND EVERYONE IS MY CUSTOMER

WHEN IS THE LAST TIME YOU conducted a business transaction with an infant? Babies are not likely to be your customer. Even if you manufacture and market baby clothes, your primary customers are the stores that buy and sell them and your secondary market are moms, fathers, family members and friends of the family. It may sound rather silly to bring up this issue, but I hear it all the time.

At networking events, in casual conversations and during meetings with prospects, I hear people state "My ideal customer is anyone" or "Everyone is my ideal customer." My response is, "Really? You've got to be joking!"

Even if your company has a vast array of customers, your ideal customers – the customers you love, love, love – are not anyone or everybody. They are your fans. They are likely to be those customers who are easy to deal with, pay on time and buy repeatedly. We have all lost money when dealing with customers who are not our fans. Those who suck away our time and energy because we hope they will buy. When they do, they are often not happy and not satisfied.

When you get to know your fans, you will be more focused on attracting more just like them. This is the power of working smarter, not harder.

Who are your ideal customers at this stage in your business?

Tip 58

SET THE BAR HIGH

WHEN I FIRST STARTED BUZZ Marketing and Consultants back in September 2000, I thought my business card and website were impressive. The logo design cost $240 and the business card printing was about $149. That's now history.

When I launched our new incorporated company, Lift Strategies, Inc., in September 2007, I made the conscious decision to set the bar high. That meant committing to an impressive new brand with an equally impressive investment. Then, in September 2008, we bolstered our website to really speak to our ideal clients and, again, this required a big financial commitment.

What are you doing to make a great first impression to your prospects? When you hand out your business card or send prospects to your website, do you get goose bumps, feel like a proud mom (or dad) or smirk with pure joy?

I attended a spectacular High Output Business Networking event and met up with business owners Debra Roed and Arthur Gemperle of Handyman franchise. Debra and Arthur own a yellow Handyman van. Previously, the company was originally known as Home Task Services and had made a so-so brand impression. Then, their head office underwent an entire rebranding process.

The new Handyman brand was impressive, fun, approachable and stands out. Debra told me that people stop just to admire their vans. Well done.

Are you excited about your brand?

Tip 59

UP IN THE AIR

OVER THE HOLIDAY SEASON, I took my daughter to see the movie *Up In The Air*, starring George Clooney. Ryan Bingham (George Clooney) is a corporate downsizer who travels around the United States firing employees.

This movie begs the question as to whether technology is the right fit for a business that is hired to fire employees on behalf of large corporations. Imagine looking at a face on a computer screen while being told you are getting fired after 20 years of service to your employer. Not such a great idea, even though the company could have saved 85% on travel costs.

Although technology is an extremely helpful tool, there is a time and a place for it.

As business owners and decision makers, we need to be able to embrace technology or we are going to lag behind our competition very quickly.

In the world of training and speaking, video conferencing and webinars are becoming a cost-effective way to gain and share new knowledge. As for business communications, staying in touch with customers using e-newsletter software like *www.constantcontact.ca* and *www.icontact.com* can be extremely effective. I use Campaign Monitor (*www.campaignmonitor.com*), which is higher priced, yet provides more statistical data than many of the newsletter solutions.

Many of the small business and franchise owners I know are currently trying to determine how to use social media as a way to communicate with their fans. This may or may not be a good fit depending on whether there is a person in place to implement using these tools effectively.

There comes a time when we need to be conscious of our ability to balance communication via technology with picking up the phone or making time for direct in-person contact with our customers and prospects. If you can manage to maintain relationships using technology as well as direct contact with your clients, then you are fully covering your bases.

Does your business have the capacity to use technology effectively to stay connected to your fans?

Tip 60

MARKETING FALLS FLAT
WITHOUT FOLLOW-UP

OVER THE YEARS, I HAVE MADE it possible for clients to experience exponential growth through an increase in "qualified" visits to their websites, a higher volume of inquiry calls and more walk-in traffic (where applicable).

Beyond this first step, where companies fall short in engaging the customer is in relationship-building and closing the sale. These days, there is no excuse for lack of follow-up or for poor sales skills because there are a number of experts in your marketplace who you can turn to for help.

It's more a matter of finding someone to work with who is the right fit for you and at the same time will push you to improve your skills and abilities. One of the best sales trainers I know is Howard Olsen.

In the city or town where you live, I'm sure there is someone – whether it be a mentor, coach or consultant – who can help you fine-tune your sales skills. One of the many valuable lessons I learned from Howard Olsen is that people do business with people they trust. Trust comes first when understanding the other person's needs, concerns or issues. Without this important foundation, it is very difficult to build a rapport.

It is our job to make the other person feel relaxed, comfortable and connected. Let's face it, even those of us with experience can have our bad days. When I haven't been out on a sales call for awhile, I definitely get nervous and this is when following a process like Howard's comes in handy. I just walk myself through the steps and do the best I can.

Like parents who have messed up – which happens often – there is always an opportunity to redeem oneself. With kids, it's about revisiting a particular issue or concern at a better time. With prospects, it's about touching base later to follow up.

Be realistic. It takes time to build relationships and determine when you can be there for the prospect with the right product or service at the right time.

Who can you ask to help you fine-tune your sales skills?

Tip 61
ENGAGE YOUR PROSPECTS

I WAS DRIVING DOWN MAIN STREET in Vancouver on a Saturday afternoon and noticed a group of enthusiastic individuals waving signs promoting a free event. It was a trade show promoting eco-friendly products. This intrigued me, so I grabbed the nearest parking spot.

I am always curious how businesses promote their products or services. This was one occasion where I could anonymously walk around and look at a number of the latest emerging eco-friendly products and see how they promoted their products. As I made my rounds, I found myself drawn towards one particular vendor. Displayed on a large metal rack were the coolest bags. This uniquely designed merchandise ranged in sizes and in applications, including large courier style, mini-courier and computer bags.

Each one was made from now defunct old billboard ads. Mike Jackson, the owner of a hip retail outlet that sells custom clothing and accessories called "Thriller," was on site to talk about his creation. His passion for these newly developed bags was contagious. What I liked most about our conversation was his interest and enthusiasm for feedback on how to make these bags even better.

Although I chose not to pull out my wallet that day, Mike had engaged me and I was hooked on the product. So before we parted ways, he gave me a small card with the same discount Thriller offered during the trade show. I would be able to use this discount when I visited his store.

I'm sure you can guess what happened next. A few months later, I showed up at Thriller and purchased three bags. I am now part of Thriller's fan club.

What are you doing to engage your prospects so they become fans?

Tip 62

BRANDING BEYOND
A LOGO

WHEN THE WORD "BRANDING" comes up in conversation, the first thing that comes to mind for many is the image of a product's or company's logo.

If we peel back the brand beyond the logo, it becomes clear that a "brand mark" is only one slice of the brand story. When a new brand is created by a design house, more often than not there is an in-depth process that takes place prior to the development of a logo or brand mark.

The process includes assessing different types of images or persona behind the organization. In some cases, a complete brand overhaul may be necessary. In my mind, the brand is the cultural impression that a business wants to present internally to its team and then externally to its customers

Last week, I was driving to a meeting. While moving slowly on a major road due to construction, I noticed a familiar van driving alongside of me. The company van had a great logo and was promoting a bottle-less drinking water system. The brand led me to believe the water tasted good and was very healthy and clean.

Just as I was thinking about this and wondering if I should call them to set up a system for my home, I saw the driver of the van throw his cigarette butt out of the window. It was still lit and fell to the ground. In this moment, I made a split decision not to call this company. Witnessing this event had tainted my impression of the brand.

I'm sure you have had a similar brand encounter that has left a bad taste in your mouth. Now it's time to ask yourself:

Is your brand driving in the right direction?

Tip 63
WHAT'S UP DOC?

REMEMBER WHEN YOU MAKE your customers happy and it results in good vibes, repeat business and satisfaction. That's definitely marketing.

Have you ever sent a client information in the form of a document and the document you send is an attachment to the e-mail? Well, when the customer saves this document, they are likely to save it to their desktop, or if they are more organized they will store it in a particular documents folder.

In my experience I have saved many documents from suppliers, then have not been able to find them on my system, and here is why. Let's say a magazine sends me their advertising rates. They decide to label the document "Jen DeTracey" or "Lift Strategies" – my name or the name of my company. When I go to look for that document at a later date on my desktop or in a folder, it is difficult to find. If the sender had labeled it "ABC rate card," I would be able to locate it immediately. Although it seems like a no-brainer, I am constantly receiving information that is labeled with my company's name, my name or my client's name instead of the subject or topic of the document.

Every time you send a document to a customer, think about what would be the best way to label the document so it is easy for the client to retrieve. The last thing you want is to get them frustrated about the proposal you sent before they even have a chance to read it.

Are you sending your clients documents that are easy for them to retrieve at a later date?

Tip 64

DO YOUR CUSTOMERS
LOVE YOUR BRAND?

WHEN YOUR BRAND COMES UP IN conversation, do people know about it? Do they know what product or service your brand specializes in, be it modern Indian fast food, fitness for women or glass repair?

If your brand is well established, this is a good thing, as long as people have a positive impression of your brand. Yet, knowing a brand and loving a brand are not the same thing. Take Apple as an example. I'm often impressed with how loyal their customers are. Every time a new product comes out – new iPod, the iPad, the latest iPhone – people flock to the stores as if they were lining up for tickets for a U2 concert.

Someone who loves a brand is a fan. Fans buy that product or service with frequency. They love the brand because they, as fans, feel special in their association with your brand. When they feel special, they tell others. In the end, your client base grows as your fans spread the word about your product or service.

Your ultimate goal should not only be to achieve brand awareness, but rather, to develop a customer base that loves your brand and becomes loyal fans of your brand. This is what builds a business and makes it successful.

Do your customers truly love your brand?

Tip 65

TRUE ESSENCE

I WAS AT ESSENCE RESTOCKING my collection of essential oils. I had brought back five empty bottles and wanted to know if they still honored a discount off the next purchase with returns.

The salesperson was alone in the store. She didn't know the answer to my question so I asked her to call another store to confirm if I could get a discount on my purchase because I was returning bottles. She was happy to oblige. As it turns out, I did get the anticipated 10% discount. When it costs $27 for a 5-ml bottle of chamomile oil, that $2.70 discount is welcomed.

While ringing in my transaction, the phone rang. I was asked if I could hold on for a moment while she took the call. During the call, the person was told the employee was the only one in the store at this moment and asked if she could take down the person's phone number and call them right back.

I was impressed with her ability to treat me and the person on the phone as important customers without compromising either relationship. As a result of her clear communication and respect, she met all my expectations of exceptional customer service.

At the time, I was reading a great book on customer service. You might be interested. It was *Exceptional Service, Exceptional Profit* by Leonardo Inghilleri and Micah Solomon.

Are you and your team doing a good job of managing customer expectations?

Tip 66

WHEN CUSTOMER
SERVICE SUCKS

LET'S FACE IT, WE'VE ALL HAD BAD customer-service experiences. We are more likely to remember these over the great ones.

For small business or franchise owners with staff, it can be a challenge to maintain the "wow" factor in the customer-service experience. I believe it starts with providing great customer-service training from day one, especially when a new employee comes on board. The next challenge is to maintain service standards on a regular basis.

It is also important to remember we are all human. Everyone has a bad day now and then. Even the best employee will have difficult days. I was in line to buy produce at a place I frequent. The customer service at this place is really hit and miss depending on the person you get and the vibe of the day.

On this particular day, the woman who was serving me was relatively new. I was curious how she was going to respond to me. Initially, there was no eye contact and her energy was low so I asked her how she was doing. After my question, she perked up slightly, looked at me and said she was struggling with her energy due to not feeling well. I acknowledged her frustration (and made a mental note to wash my vegetables when I got home) and ended up having a lovely conversation with her for the rest of the transaction. She even gave me a complimentary organic apple that had not made it on to the scale when she was ringing in my order.

My point is this: We often get what we anticipate is going to happen. If we think someone is going to give us crappy service, it is very possible they will. When we take the time to connect with the person who is helping us and treat them like they are more than a number – that we truly care about our interaction with them – the likelihood of a great customer-service experience can be much higher.

Are you maintaining exceptional interaction with staff, contractors and those you buy from and sell to?

Tip 67

MAKING PEOPLE
FEEL GOOD

ONE OF THE SIMPLEST WAYS TO market to others is to make them feel good. Sending a thank you card, flowers or taking someone to lunch are great ways to give back to those who've helped you in some way. They may have passed along a referral that generated new business or given you advice that ultimately led to securing a new client contract. When we acknowledge and express appreciation to others, not only do they feel good, so do we.

This type of marketing comes from the heart.

I attended an important sales meeting where I was outlining how working with my company would benefit this client-to-be. The meeting was a big challenge for me and until the moment I wrote this tip, I didn't know the final outcome.

What I did know was how critical it was to follow up with the decision maker(s). That night, after flying home from the meeting, despite feeling exhausted, I sat down and wrote personalized note cards to each of the management team. The note cards acknowledged each individual's contribution to the meeting and told him/her how I was looking forward to working with them.

Believe it or not, even though following up sounds like a simple thing to do, many people do not take the time to express their appreciation to others in a very special way.

What steps can you take to acknowledge those who have helped move your business forward or those who will soon be contributing to growing your bottom line?

Tip 68

DOG FRIENDLY ADVANTAGE

THE BEST THING ABOUT THE economy right now is how creative we marketing people can be, especially when clients have tight marketing budgets. At Lift Strategies, we know our clients have great ideas; often it is our job to help them determine the logistics and time frame in which to best put their ideas into action.

Here's a very cool idea that required a very small financial investment. Its concept was developed by one of our clients' marketing coordinator from Vancouver Gas Fireplaces.

The owner of Vancouver Gas Fireplaces often brings his dog to work. This means the place is set up as a dog friendly environment, including a dog dish that automatically refills with water.

The marketing coordinator decided to use this as a promotional opportunity. She had vinyl artwork put on the front door that said "Pet Friendly" with a line extending below the text to a dog door and paw prints. The marketing coordinator also added the "Pet Friendly" information to the contact page on the company website. Last, she approached a number of the local directories that post information about pet friendly places. Some of these sites added Vancouver Gas Fireplaces to their listings.

Do you have a marketing idea that barks outside of the box?

Tip 69
GREAT CUSTOMER SERVICE

I RECEIVED A FLYER AND SAMPLE in the mail offering an amazing deal to first-time customers for high-quality promotional pens.

At first, I couldn't believe that this was a legitimate offer. I went to the company's website and looked at the products and their ordering system to make sure I felt comfortable proceeding.

From the get go, what grabbed me about the sample pen was its color. Remember, we do buy primarily based on emotions. The color of the pen was a perfect fit with Lift Strategies' corporate colors.

I placed my order, and received a proof and an e-mail stating the pens would be shipped in a few days. Impressive.

When all 1,000 of the pens arrived, I was very excited. This was the first time I had invested in a promotional product for Lift Strategies. I opened the box, confirmed the website address was correct. Later, I discovered the phone number was not. Imagine me doing a speech about the importance of branding and then handing everyone a pen and telling them to scratch off the incorrect phone number? Not good.

At first, I was worried that it was my error because of my dyslexia. I was preparing to suck it up. Fortunately, when I double-checked the e-mails and my proof from the supplier, I learned the error was not mine. My relief was immeasurable. The company was incredibly responsive to the situation and turned around a new set of pens within 48 hours. Now that's great customer service.

When your business makes an error, how quickly does it get corrected?

Tip 70

ABOVE AND BEYOND – CUSTOMER SERVICE

HOPEFULLY THE ANSWER TO THE question "Who do you love?" is your customers; in other words, your fan club.

Although I can't recall the origin of this statement, I do believe it to be true. The number one reason customers don't continue to buy from the same source is because they believe the person or company they are purchasing from doesn't care about them.

When my dog Jupiter was alive, I bought his pet food from Woofgang Pet Supplies. There was an occasion when I called the owner and asked if he could personally deliver the food because Jupiter was very ill. Jupiter had eaten something poisonous while at my cabin and I was unsure if he was going to make it through.

Without hesitation, Raymond came that night after his store closed. Jupiter greeted him with kisses despite feeling very sick. It was a very happy moment.

That week it would have been difficult for me to get to the store to buy his regular supply of raw food. It's not something I could just pick up anywhere. Although Jupiter was not eating at the time, I had to believe that at some point he would return to his regular, insatiable eating habits.

Raymond understood the importance of maintaining and servicing his fan club. Because of the exceptional service and care that I receive from Raymond at Woofgang, I remain a loyal fan.

This story has a happy ending. Jupiter recovered after two weeks. I was grateful beyond belief for the many amazing individuals who comprised Jupiter's fan club and did whatever they could to bring him back to good health.

How can you go above and beyond for your biggest fans?

Tip 71

COLLABORATIVE PARTNERS AND CONNECTIONS

I HAVE KNOWN STEVE THOMPSON, the Marketing and Merchandising Manager for Pharmasave Drugs Pacific Office, for over ten years. Over that time, he and I have crossed paths in several capacities. In 2010, I told him about how the British Columbia government was providing grant money to businesses for training. One of the types of training they were funding was my LIFFT® Training program. Steve was well aware of the work I did to enhance their marketing efforts with the management team at one of their franchisee locations.

As a result of our conversation, Steve asked me to send him a flier with the details of the grant and the training program. He offered to send it to all the stores in British Columbia. The day the information hit Pharmasave's intranet, I received a call from a front store manager who picked a date for the training and submitted the grant application.

Not only is Steve Thompson a wonderful person and good at what he does, he is also an ideal person for me to collaborate with. He recognized the benefits of the program and wanted to make it accessible to the stores he works with. Based on my experience with retailers and my background in the pharmacy industry many years ago, this arrangement proved to be a perfect fit.

Collaboration can be a highly effective way to help others and generate more business in the process. Think about the people you know.

Who could you collaborate with to generate a win-win outcome for both parties?

Tip 72

AWARD WINNING STRATEGIES

SERENA RYDER, A CANADIAN POP music artist from Ontario, won a prestigious Juno Award for Adult Alternative Album of the Year in 2009. I had the opportunity to attend her show at the Stanley Theatre the following night. All I can say is, "Wow!" Because of my history in the music business, I have seen many rock concerts. Many were good but I've seen an equal number that were bad. I am most impressed with the performers when they make a conscious effort to connect with their audience in a deep and meaningful way beyond singing their songs. In my opinion, it is the lead singer's responsibility to give the audience an emotional and memorable experience.

In a nutshell, this means customer service beyond expectations.

Serena Ryder delivered. Not only did she start out by having a great conversation with us, her audience, she was also funny, energetic and engaging. She gave 150%. We were right there with her every step of the way.

Obviously music has the power to bring forth a deep connection, so how can we apply this concept to our business? If you own a retail business, selecting the right music at your location can be critical in keeping customers in your store or driving them out the door too quickly.

Conversely, your small business or franchise may have a different business model where music doesn't apply. From this perspective, it comes down to creating the ideal atmosphere for doing business with your clients. This could be as simple as meeting at a restaurant that your client enjoys or having a meeting in an environment that is comfortable without too many distractions.

What can you do to ensure your customer's environment puts them at ease and deepens your connection with them?

Part Three

ADDITIONAL
INSIGHTS

Tip 73

AUTOMATED WORLD

THE MORE SPEAKING ENGAGEMENTS I do, the more I travel. Through traveling I have discovered how many things are automated, even compared to a few years back.

I used to get excited about getting a paper towel from an automated dispenser in public bathrooms and now things have gone beyond that.

At the beginning of June in 2009, I was staying at the amazing and beautiful Crest Hotel in Prince Rupert. To my surprise, when I left the public washroom on the main floor, the door automatically opened for me. I have to admit the first few times it happened, I found it rather trippy. After that, I appreciated and came to expect the convenience.

Back when I was 14, on vacation in Florida with my family, I stuck my hand inside a pop machine. With only a few scratches, I was able to retrieve a free can of pop. Nowadays, the beverage machines at most airports are so automated that a mechanical arm grabs the bottle of your choice and delivers it to an automated door.

When this tip was sent out as an e-mail, it was scheduled well in advance of when it actually arrived to each person's inbox. This is the beauty of automation.

Isn't it time you found tools to automate some of your marketing initiatives?

Tip 74

GETTING OURSELVES
BACK TO THE GARDEN

AT ONE OF MY REGULAR NETWORKING events, Nancy Eagles* from Inanna Herbal Remedies ended her 90-second sales pitch with the slogan, "We've got to get ourselves back to the garden" – a line from Joni Mitchell's song *Woodstock*.

Nancy recognized how this line fits so well with what she does. She creates natural products using natural herbs hand-picked from wild gardens around British Columbia.

When I heard this slogan, I asked myself, "How does this apply to me and all the other business professionals at this networking meeting?" The first thing that entered my mind was the importance of "walking our talk." All of us at this meeting were experts in at least one specific area. How were we getting ourselves back to our gardens? In my mind, that meant asking myself this crucial question, "How am I living and applying the advice I deliver to my clients on a regular basis?"

Am I following the 5-Step LIFFT® Process I expect my clients to implement? Am I actively marketing my business? Do I use the layer approach? Am I committed to following up? Do I track results? Is my core message in line with the type of clients I want to continue working with?

I can proudly say, "Yes."

———

Are you applying the advice you give your clients to your own business?

*Unfortunately, Nancy Eagles passed away suddenly less than a year after I wrote this tip. I would like to dedicate this tip to her.

Tip 75

TEMPTATION
IS COSTLY

MOST ORGANIZATIONS UNDERSTAND the value of marketing and sales. Yet, one of the biggest challenges is to not be tempted by a "great deal."

I was speaking at the Women Mean Business Conference in Chilliwack. After the event was over I headed to my cabin in Yale, British Columbia. When I arrived, despite it being very hot outside, inside it was cold and damp. As the sun dropped behind the mountain, I started to build a fire. Although I was eager to take off the chill as quickly as possible with a roaring blaze, I diligently took steps to get the twigs burning into red hot flames before adding small logs. At the time, I knew the ultimate benefit would be an awesome fire within 15 minutes. After that my efforts would be minimal – just adding a medium to large log every 30-60 minutes.

During the past two decades as a small business growth expert, I have noticed business owners and their teams struggle, looking for a quick marketing fix guaranteed to provide a big payoff. Invariably, an advertising sales rep will call and offer "an amazing, not to be missed deal." In that moment, it is so easy to be tempted by such a great promise.

The best way to avoid falling into this trap is to develop and implement an annual marketing action plan. When you do this, you can easily determine whether each opportunity supports your annual objectives or not. Avoid being clouded by "the deal of a lifetime."

What are you going to say the next time an advertising sales rep offers you the "best deal ever?"

Tip 76

WHAT IS THE
REAL ISSUE?

I HAD A PROSPECT CONTACT ME about needing help with marketing their business. Upon talking to this client about their urgent need to generate more sales for their company, I discovered that marketing was not the issue. In fact, they had done a good job of marketing to drive traffic to their business.

The problem they faced was marketing to attract the right employees. When a small business in the service sector needs people with a specific expertise who are committed to show up and they don't, this can kill a business. In small communities, reliable, skilled employees can be even more difficult to find.

Take, for example, a massage therapy clinic or spa that employs three or more staff. If a client has an appointment booked and receives a call saying the appointment has to be postponed, this can really damage the reputation of a company. It's not easy to find a substitute at the last minute in small communities, let alone a large city. Additionally, the customer will likely not want a replacement.

Before you conclude you need help with marketing your company, take a look at the other issues at hand. It is possible that you may have a management issue or a human relations concern that needs to be dealt with before investing in actively marketing your business.

What is the core issue your business is presently struggling with?

Tip 77

THE SALES FLIP – TURNING SALES ENQUIRIES INTO OPPORTUNITIES

HOW MANY TIMES HAVE YOU received a sales call from someone enquiring about doing business with you? This happens to me regularly and since I love to help others, I take the time to listen to what they have to say. Once I know what they want, I can decide whether it is in either of our best interests to continue the conversation.

I remember being contacted by a sales trainer. He wanted to know if his services would be suitable for my business.

In this case, I was very intrigued by what the sales trainer was saying and through speaking with him, I discovered that he had done business with a prospect I had been trying to make contact with for several weeks. When I mentioned this to him, he told me who would be the best person to contact. As it turned out, this was not the same person I'd been calling. Had I blown off the conversation with this sales trainer, I never would have found out this valuable piece of information. To top it off, the sales trainer also gave me a lead on another company that I pursued.

Opportunities come in unexpected places. The next time you get a call from someone who wants to sell you something, find out how you can help them and then ask how they can help you.

How many conversations can you turn into meaningful connections?

Tip 78

CONSISTENCY COUNTS – PART 1

A CLOSE FRIEND OF MINE regularly stops at her local fast food drive-thru for breakfast. Last week she asked for a cup of hot water with her order. The woman at the window told her that request would cost her 15¢. In the past, there was no charge for this "little extra." Yet, on this particular day, the woman asked for money and clarified that the 15¢ was to cover the cost of the disposable cup and lid.

Any of us in business know that this makes sense. It costs the restaurant money to provide water in a disposable cup to its customers. The next day my friend returned and was serviced by the same woman. She ordered the same breakfast, requested hot water, then proceeded to hand over an empty travel mug.

Despite the fact that there was no disposable cup and lid being used, the woman still charged her for the hot water. It's difficult to know what this restaurant's policy is. If they have one, it is inconsistent. If it happened to my friend, how many other people are experiencing the same scenario?

If you create a new policy in your company that impacts your customers, be sure to communicate this policy clearly to all employees. Customers like and expect consistency. They are also willing to pay a little extra to get it.

What policies do you need to communicate to your employees?

Tip 79

CONSISTENCY COUNTS – PART 2

ONE AFTERNOON I WAS DRIVING home from a number of client meetings and my attention was drawn towards a small wooden building at the top of a hill. With all the hype of the 2010 Winter Games in Vancouver at the time, it was cool to see so many businesses donning Canadian flags, putting up signage that said "Go Canada" and decorating their storefronts accordingly.

The particular building that caught my eye was a sign company I had worked with on several occasions. They had cleverly taken advantage of their red building and placed a white maple leaf in the center close to the roof. It looked great!

On a cement wall beside the building was a beautifully created red banner with the company's logo. The logo was white and three dimensional. It was outstanding and caught my eye immediately.

When I looked more closely at the building and its surroundings on the industrial street, I noticed a more traditional sign that sat on the lawn of the property. It was white, framed in brown wood. The problem with their sign was that it stood out like a sore thumb because it was so dirty. It's hard to know whether they were too lazy to clean it or if the black and grey streaks were permanent due to the aging and weather conditions.

If I was a prospect who was considering using this sign company's services and I saw the inconsistency in the quality of their outdoor signs, I would think about going somewhere else. After all, I want to know I'm going to get a great looking sign that will be able to withstand the ravages of time and all sorts of weather.

Is there consistency in the way you present your company and its brand?

Tip 80
BIG BUSINESS GOES GUERRILLA

I WAS WALKING TO A CLIENT meeting in the downtown core. Out of the corner of my eye I spotted some funny business. Standing at one of the newspaper box dispensers were two young women who looked like they were up to no good.

From almost half a block away, their bright red T-shirts stood out as they started to take copies of the *Georgia Straight* (Vancouver weekly entertainment news) out of the newspaper box while guiltily looking around. As I got closer, I witnessed them inserting a red promotional card into each copy. While passing by, I caught a glance of the logo on their T-shirts. It was the logo of Blackberry, the smartphone company.

As a guerrilla marketing strategist who gets my clients the biggest bang for their marketing buck, I was uncertain of Blackberry's motivation in this case. Would it not have been cheaper to simply pay the *Georgia Straight* to insert the promotional card into that week's edition?

To this day I don't know if the young women were steering away from the original directive by trying to offload the cards instead of handing them out to the public.

What I do know is if your small business or franchise chooses to take a guerrilla approach to its marketing initiatives, you must start by setting a clear objective. Then, devise a tactical plan that is easy to implement and has a high probability of achieving the outcome you desire.

Do you have a method to your marketing madness?

Tip 81

COMPETITIVE EDGE

EVERY TIME I'M SHOPPING downtown in Vancouver, I love to walk by the foodie hot spots with long lineups. A place that keeps grabbing my attention is a hotdog stand on the corner of Burrard and Smithe, right outside the Sutton Place Hotel.

Unlike other hotdog stands in the downtown core, this one always has long lineups of customers congregating around a red hotdog cart. Japadog was started by a world hotdog-eating champion, Takeru Kabayashi. Unlike any other hotdog stands in the city, the mix of condiments hotdog enthusiasts can choose from at Japadog are quite novel.

For example, the Misomayo hotdog comes with a turkey sausage, radish sprouts, sesame miso and Japanese mayo. The Oroshi is a bratwurst with green onions, grated daikon, teriyaki sauce and nori.

Takeru Kabayashi's radical idea has become a profitable and growing business endeavor.

Most of you who are reading this tip may already have an established business. Whether your ideas are radical or not, it is important to find ways to differentiate your business from your competition. Not only does Takeru now have many hotdog carts around Vancouver, he has a restaurant and take out window on one of the busiest foot traffic streets in town.

Once you determine what core aspects of your business are unique from others, you can develop clear and dynamic messaging that will attract the customers you love.

What makes your business truly unique from your competition?

Tip 82
GIVING MORE VALUE

THERE ARE A GREAT NUMBER OF business associations and chambers of commerce that provide marketing and/or lobbying services to their members. As an expert who speaks professionally, I am often asked to speak at association events across Canada.

One Monday morning, I was in Hope, British Columbia, presenting my new keynote speech, "Get Your Business Rockin'...Building a Loyal Fan Club During Challenging Times." This event was hosted by the Hope Chamber of Commerce.

I was particularly blown away by the commitment of the Hope Chamber of Commerce to help their members sustain and gain their businesses. The Hope Chamber recognized the value of bringing me in to present to their members. They also recognized that the "Five Marketing Essentials to Getting 50% More LIFFT® for Your Business" full-day training program would benefit local businesses.

Because of the Hope Chamber's commitment to support their members and provide exceptional value, they chose to subsidize 27% of the event's budget, host the venue and provide lunch. If that isn't going above and beyond, I don't know what is.

What are you doing to provide exceptional value to your top customers? After all, your top customers are your number one fans. You definitely want to give them a good reason to return to buy more and more often.

What is one thing you can do this month to give more value to your fans?

Tip 83

POWER OF
THE PEOPLE

LIKE MANY BUSINESS OWNERS, I like to give back to my local community. One of the events I attend is the "Empty Bowl Project," hosted by A Loving Spoonful.

A Loving Spoonful provides meals to those living with HIV/AIDS. Meals are delivered by a large and enthusiastic community of volunteers.

When I purchased my ticket for this fundraising event, a ticket was mailed to my office without a service charge. Two weeks later, I received a personally handwritten card from A Loving Spoonful volunteers thanking me for buying a ticket to the event.

The day before the event, I was contacted by phone by a volunteer who wanted to confirm that I had received my ticket. When I asked what the dress code was for this event, I was put on hold and the volunteer found out the details and got back to me immediately.

Of all the events I have attended, whether for profit or not, the customer service has never been as impressive as what I experienced with A Loving Spoonful.

What is your organization doing to provide the best customer service possible to your fans (volunteers, employees, customers, donors, suppliers and collaborating partners)?

Tip 84

GIVE MORE,
MAKE MORE

I WAS SCHEDULED TO ATTEND AN evening board meeting for one of the organizations I volunteer for. My plan was to drive my car to Pilates class (which was only three blocks away), then go right to my meeting. By taking the car, I would be saving enough time to do both activities without compromising either one.

On my way to class, I realized I had a flat tire. I immediately headed back home and called CAA (Canadian Automobile Association). The mechanic arrived within 30 minutes of my call and in seconds found a small screw had punctured my tire. He informed me of a service CAA has been providing since November of 2006; CAA offers members the option of having their tires plugged for only $15.00 each.

This solution of inserting a special rubber plug to seal punctured tires has been proven successful by the American Automobile Association. I was grateful that CAA had added this service to their roster because, within five minutes, my tire was repaired. I missed my Pilates class, yet was on time for the board meeting. The tire plugging service was a win-win for me and CAA. It saved me from having to drive on a spare and needing to visit the garage for repair and balancing. CAA saved themselves the time required to switch over to a spare tire, and they made more money in the process.

What proven products or services can you add to your roster that will save your customers time, stress and/or money while increasing your bottom line?

Tip 85

COPY CAT CUPCAKERY – PART 1

MANY YEARS AGO, I WAS WALKING down Denman Street in Vancouver with a client. We passed by Cupcakes, a little bakery that specialized in small and large cupcakes with "real" butter icing.

My client said, "They will never survive."

In my head, I thought, "Wow, what a great idea to specialize in cupcakes!"

Growing up I always loved cupcakes because they are so much fun to look at and eat. The retail store was so colorful with beautiful round platters on stands filled with cupcakes and enclosed in a see-through plastic lid.

Since that day on Denman Street, Cupcakes has been very successful and has multiple franchise locations throughout North America.

More recently, I noticed a new business that was in the process of opening on Commercial Drive in one of Vancouver's hip bohemian neighborhoods. The business was Cassia Cupcakery. This did not surprise me at all. In fact, since I saw the first Cupcakes location on Denman Street, I knew the business concept was going to be big. Cassia Cupcakery is just one of the many copycats that will ride the wave of this exciting concept.

There is always room for competition in the market when a great concept meets with favorable demand. Developing a business concept takes a great deal of time, money and energy, but can be extremely rewarding. Taking an existing idea and seeing your vision become a reality can be just as rewarding.

What is your path to launch a new concept or take a successful concept and launch it in a new region?

Tip 86

CUPCAKERY – PART 2

IN THE LAST TIP, I WROTE ABOUT Cassia Cupcakery and how they copied the very successful idea of Vancouver-based Cupcakes.

Cupcakes' successful growth will do them well. The question is, can they be responsive to the demands of the marketplace as they continue to grow their franchise operation?

When I was writing the first of these two tips about Cassia Cupcakery, I was conducting research online. At that time, I could not find their website so I'm assuming they don't have one yet. What I did discover was a number of postings on a blogging site called Yelp where people rate and comment on businesses they like and dislike. There were several comments about Cassia Cupcakery. One woman noted that since Cassia Cupcakery is located on Commercial Drive – the land of many who enjoy a vegan diet – she was very interested in whether the bakery offered vegan cupcakes.

Right away, I wondered to myself, "Will the owner of Cassia Cupcakery find out about this request? If they do, how responsive will they be to it?"

To my delight, as I walked by Cassia Cupcakery the following month, I noticed a bold message on their sandwich board: "Now, try our new Vegan Cupcakes."

Well done, Cassia Cupcakery. Everyone is happy when business owners take the fans at a specific location or region seriously. The fans get their vegan cupcakes and the staff and their associates get happy customers, which leads to positive word-of-mouth. And best of all, there will be more money in Cassia Cupcakery's piggy bank.

How responsive are you being to your fans' requests?

Tip 87
DO YOU WANT
MY BUSINESS?

I WENT TO MY NEIGHBORHOOD Rogers Video with the mission to rent the movie *127 Hours*. As I was walking around the store, I could not find a copy anywhere.

I proceeded to approach the front desk and asked one of the two sales staff if they had a copy in stock. I was told they didn't. Then I requested that they put one on hold for me when it arrived and give me a call. According to policy, this was not possible. I was welcome to call them or come back to the store. At that point I asked for their phone number and the sales guy reticently handed me a business card and gave me the clear impression that there was no guarantee that I would get a copy.

As I was leaving the video store, I called my friend to share my disappointment with her, at which point she told me she could simply order it on demand from her local cable provider. Perfect. Rogers lost the opportunity to have my business. I would have returned to the store and picked up a copy of *127 Hours* if they had simply offered to call me and tell me that I would be able to get the movie for that evening.

Rogers Video needs to think differently about its approach. Video stores are folding because people can now borrow DVDs from their local library, order through Netflix or on-demand through their cable provider. We live in a society where people do not want to have to work to be your customers, nor should they have to.

Ironically, since this tip was written, Rogers Video has closed a number of stores.

How are you making it easy for your customers and prospects to pull out their wallet?

Tip 88

CAN'T BEAT THE REAL THING

BACK IN DECEMBER SEVERAL years ago now, I received the following e-mail from a client in Toronto I worked with:

> Hi Jen
>
> Just received your Christmas card … and while last Christmas I had about 25 Christmas cards displayed on my office door, this year I currently have 4 displayed on my door … but I've had lots and lots of e-Christmas cards.
>
> So … this is just a long-winded way to say thank you for the good, old-fashioned, traditional Christmas card. It's much appreciated."

There is something to be said for making an impression by not following trends. I personally love opening cards when they come in the mail. Let's face it, when people receive their mail, those envelopes that don't resemble a bill or an invoice are definitely more appealing. When the name and address is hand-written the impact is even greater.

With less mail being sent and more electronic communication taking place, personal cards will continue to be more and more memorable.

Are you sending personalized cards through the post to your clients and prospects?

Tip 89

GET REAL
WITH YOURSELF

DO YOU EVER FEEL LIKE YOUR work pile is growing and it's difficult to stay on top of everything?

I do. Usually, when this happens, I pull back long enough to get my personal and business houses in order so I can move forward with more ease. I have to admit, as someone who likes to keep busy and do the work I love to do, this is not an easy task for me.

I came back from a speaking tour and ended up in the hospital due to difficulties with motor skills on the left side of my body. I remember attending a play with my friends. Over the course of the evening they said, "That's it. We are taking you to emergency."

As it turns out, I had inflammation of the brain and needed several intensive treatments over the course of three days to resolve the issue. Fortunately, I had a full and speedy recovery. Although I am still feeling the effects of what happened, I am grateful to be able to walk normally and use my left hand as I could before.

This was a wake-up call for me. I'm sure many of you have experienced a set back either in your personal life or your health that has deeply affected you. Dealing with unexpected personal or health issues can be shocking. I remind myself daily what Eckhart Tolle says, "Life will give you whatever experiences are most helpful for the evolution of your consciousness."

This experience has reaffirmed what I value the most. I value my time, my loved ones and family, doing what I love, and being of service to others in my areas of expertise.

How can you take what you value most and apply that to be the best person you can for yourself and your business?

MAKING THINGS HAPPEN

WHEN LIFE GETS BUSY, IT BECOMES challenging to know what to make a priority. As I learned early in business ownership, if I didn't map out my holidays well in advance, they didn't happen. The same applies to moving your business forward.

The first step to marketing and creating awareness for your company is to set aside time to focus specifically on this aspect of your business, just like you would schedule time to meet with suppliers or conduct a conference call. Allocate time every week, or every day if that works better for you, to invest time for planning the promotion of your business. Commit to scheduling time in advance just like you would a meeting. Plan to do this at the beginning of every month.

The second step is to find a suitable place where you can concentrate without interruptions. You will be more productive and it will take less of your time to get things done. Not all of your time will be planning in solitude, yet this incubation time can be precious. You may need feedback from others as part of this process. This may include scheduling time with your team; a consultant and/or marketing providers will likely be part of this course of action.

Once you are certain about what you want to do, the third step is to develop a timeline and action plan. In fact, this is the most important step. It will be easier to communicate to all concerned once you have this in place. Communication and management of each concept is critical for the best outcome.

I recommend you start with one marketing or customer service idea and get it up and running successfully before initiating another. It is better to properly implement one concept than have five half-baked ideas floating around generating no impact. As you successfully implement one concept, you can then get another one up and running. I call this "stacking." The stacking process allows room for one or more ideas or concepts to fail without becoming a problem because you will eventually have many methods in place to promote your company and keep your customers coming back for more.

Over time, the impact of your efforts will be created through multiple initiatives. This is when you will begin to witness greater customer engagement and growing profits.

I hope this book has inspired you to view your customers, brand and business from different perspectives or reinforce what you have been thinking but not fully living. By doing this, you may be surprised how much easier it becomes to set priorities, promote your products and/or services, gain more customers and generate more profits.

When you have passion for what you do and the right systems in place to make it happen, it is amazing how focusing on the "right things" becomes second nature.

I wish you good fortune and continued personal discovery as you take the next steps towards what continues to be an unfolding journey.

ABOUT THE AUTHOR

JEN DeTRACEY is a strategic alchemist and one of Canada's top marketing experts. She is an author, professional speaker and small business growth consultant. Jen has more than two decades of strategic marketing experience.

Jen is also the founder of Lift Strategies Inc. Prior to Lift Strategies, she owned and operated Buzz Marketing and Consultants.

Jen developed the LIFFT® Process. LIFFT® is a proven five-step strategic marketing process that helps small businesses accelerate their growth, and manage that growth without overextending their people and their resources.

Prior to business ownership, Jen was the VP of Marketing for Sarah McLachlan's record label Nettwerk Records. She then joined the Virgin Entertainment Group and was part of the team that launched Canada's first Virgin Megastore in Vancouver. Jen worked with the buyers and management of Virgin to promote and generate exceptional revenues for one of Canada's most dynamic retail operations.

Jen works with small business and franchise owners across a broad spectrum of industries and delivers keynotes regularly at conferences and conventions. She has developed workshops and training programs geared towards helping small business owners focus on creating and implementing effective marketing systems and action plans.

Jen's vision is to connect with an infinite number of business owners, leaders and creators through her books, training and keynotes to assist them in creating the framework to actualize their dreams.

To contact Jen DeTracey for consulting, keynote speeches and training programs:

Toll Free: 1-877-255-2098

Tel: 604-255-2098

liftstrategies.com